THE LAST ADVENTURER

THE LAST ADVENTURER

MESSAGE IN A BOTTLE

A memoir of
Fons Oerlemans and Kee Arens

Medina Publishing

First published in 2023 by Medina Publishing Ltd
50 High Street
Cowes
Isle of Wight
PO31 7RR
England

www.medinapublishing.com

Printed and bound in the UK by Clays Elcograf S.p.A.

ISBN Hardback: 978-1-911487-89-0

Fons Oerlemans and Kee Arens assert their moral right to be
identified as the authors of this book.

CIP data: A catalogue record for this book is available at the
British Library.

Cover designed by Kimi Holden Huang
Edited by Rachel Hamilton
Layout by Alexandra Lawson
Reprographics by wotUwant

Photography courtesy of Fons Oerlemans

Typeset in 11 / 16 pt Athelas

Printed and bound in Great Britain by Clays Ltd, Elcograf S.pA.
Medina Publishing is committed to a sustainable future for
our business, our readers, and our planet. This book is made from
Forest Stewardship Council ® certified paper.

MIX
Paper | Supporting
responsible forestry
FSC
www.fsc.org
FSC® C018072

To Kee, my wife and anchor.

*May these pages hold our memories,
as the tides of time slowly
carry away your own.*

Contents

Throughout the book, Fons and Kee invariably express distances in nautical miles with speed in knots. Elsewhere, they use the metric system.

Introduction

On 14 August 2023, Fons Oerlemans took the helm of *Message in a Bottle* and cast off from her mooring in Antwerp's Kempischdok. The journey was planned as a 30-minute passage to deliver this unique creation to the educational trust, Stormkop, at their harbour adjacent to the Scheldt River. There, as captain, Fons would guide the vessel into her new home.

Although his wife, Kee, couldn't accompany him on this short, watershed trip, she had been by his side throughout the transformation of a simple metal cylinder into a high-speed hydrofoil they named *Flying Bottle*. Recognised as the first woman to cross the Atlantic Ocean on a raft with Fons, Kee was his fearless partner on other crossings, including their last journey on the renamed and repurposed *Message in a Bottle*. Upon their return, the vessel became their home for 11 years, serving as a daily reminder of their shared adventures.

After a few wrong turns and delays caused by tidal fluctuations and low bridges, Fons and his crew safely navigated *Message in a Bottle* to her new berth at Stormkop. Their arrival was celebrated by the cheers of the 300-strong crowd that had gathered to welcome Fons and his craft – a testament to their incredible history and its unique design and original purpose. Here, *Message in a Bottle* would begin her next adventure as a hub for education, demonstrations and exhibitions for all generations.

For Fons, Kee and *Message in a Bottle,* the voyage continues. This is more than just an account of Atlantic crossings. It's the story of two remarkable lives: of Fons and Kee and the dreams they've dreamt and challenges they've overcome making four Atlantic Ocean crossings in four wildly different, yet equally remarkable, vessels.

Fons is an adventurer, inventor, designer, engineer, builder, navigator, aviator and sailor of incredible ambition. While some of his dreams remained elusive, perhaps fortunately in the case of his plans for a record free-fall from a balloon at 44,000 metres – although he did design and construct the aluminium gondola *Apollo 19* and was confident of its viability – other innovations like his gyroscopes and the world's smallest helicopter were successfully built and flown.

With the exception of the life raft, *Atlantis*, each of his extraordinary floating contraptions took years to dream up, plan and complete and was more than just a mode of transport. These were inspired labours of love, designed and constructed with integrity and tested to survive the forces of the Atlantic. *Last Generation*, *Seaview*, *Floating Truck* and *Message in a Bottle* all took their crew safely across the ocean. Today, both *Message in Bottle* and the scale prototype of *Flying Bottle* still survive to inspire a future generation of innovators, risk takers and adventurers and help teach the skills essential to bring dreams to life.

As we delve into these pages, the vast ocean becomes a backdrop to the indomitable spirit of two extraordinary lives, woven together by creativity, adventure and an enduring love.

Peter Harrigan
Cowes, Isle of Wight
August 2023

Early Days
Battlefield Beginnings

1944, German-occupied Belgium might not seem the obvious inspiration for a lifetime of innovation and exploration. But in the fourth year of the Second World War, as a six-year-old living in the small village of Nieuwmoer about 35 kilometres north of Antwerp, I was regularly brought face to face with the raw power of human invention.

Some of my earliest memories are of war machines camouflaged in the woods and fields around us. Enemy soldiers used bushes and nets to hide mighty Panther and Tiger tanks, anti-aircraft guns and heavy machine guns from the Allied air forces. As squadrons of B17-Flying Fortresses and Lancasters roared over my village, aimed at the heart of Germany, the German anti-aircraft guns unleashed a barrage of glowing grenades into the sky. These grenades exploded in mid-air, forming dark clouds that dissipated between the bombers. The soldiers covered the smoking cannon barrels with camouflage nets whenever venomous, low-flying Thunderbolts or Spitfires discovered the cannons' muzzle flashes. The 20-millimetre gun located in our garden would swing upwards and hurl glowing metal in the direction of the hunting aircraft.

As the German gunners dived into the depths of their trenches, we ran for cover in our bomb shelter, a two-metre-deep room dug by my father and covered with wooden planks and soil. Anyone whose house did not have a concrete basement had to build a shelter to protect occupants from bullets and flying shrapnel. However, nothing could protect you against a direct hit, such as the 230-kilogram, 2.2-metre-long MK 82 bomb that landed on one house in our neighbourhood. All the residents that had sought shelter in their cellar died immediately.

Crashing aeroplanes were a regular phenomenon in our village. Broken and battered bombers limping back home to England sparked my fascination with engineering and the mechanics of movement. I collected remnants from the wreckage, not as sinister souvenirs but as sources of revelation. I was intrigued by the power held within the machines of war, their ability to displace air and defy gravity, the engineering that powered them and the human will that drove them forward. I was also captivated by the ingenuity on display. We discovered thousands of silver paper bundles dropped by Allied bombers. We later learnt that the British had developed this countermeasure – known as chaff – to cast reflections and generate false echoes that would confuse the German air defence's radar-guided cannons.

Fons 1945

We were in constant danger from mines, rogue ammunition, bombing and Germans who shot at anything that moved. Each day it became more difficult for us to attend our village school. War brought out the worst in humanity. But it also showed me the resilience of the human spirit in men like my father, picked up during the dark days of 1943 and sent to Northern France to work in the complex maze of bunkers that formed part of General Rommel's Atlantic Wall. To slow down the Nazi operation, he and his fellow enslaved Europeans adopted a strategy of minimal cooperation. However, they had to be careful not to be labelled as saboteurs, as such accusations could have earned them a place in front of a firing squad.

After months of hard labour, the Germans granted my father one week's leave. During this respite, he went into hiding with several other objectors, seeking refuge in various houses within our village. He had to be constantly vigilant because at any moment the secret police could arrest him and send him to a concentration camp. The dreaded Gestapo mostly carried out their raids in the middle of the night and my mother and I had to endure three of these brutal and surprise visits.

My father's stories, shared on long winter nights as we gathered around the groaning, glowing pot-bellied stove, filled my young mind with tales of heroism. They ignited in me a desire to conquer the elements and face any peril that lay ahead. My thoughts always turned to the sea rather than the land. Something about the sea lured me as I listened to the adventures of brave local smugglers and sailors. I could hardly dare to breathe as I imagined the vessels I could build – sturdy rafts and seaworthy boats that could navigate treacherous waters and withstand the most powerful waves, with me at the helm.

As Canadian and British soldiers freed Antwerp's port, the front line moved steadily closer. With truckloads of explosives, the Germans destroyed our beautiful old buildings and made enormous holes in our bumpy main street to halt the advancing tanks. The Long Toms, the British long-distance cannons, targeted the German fortifications in our village, blasting big holes in houses and bars. After the war, it turned out that not a single tree in our area was suitable for sawing into planks. The trunks were all full of bullets and shrapnel from grenades.

Five years earlier, in May 1940, the German army had stormed in triumphantly with the most modern war equipment in an unstoppable blitzkrieg. Now, they fled the conquered areas on horseback, foot or bicycle, taking every opportunity to burn buildings and terrorise civilians as they passed. Few houses were left unscathed by grenade explosions, fires and looting. Many people were beaten or needlessly killed.

When the freedom fighters reached our area, intense battles caused heavy losses on both sides. All day long, we heard the rattling of light weapons, explosions, and the barking of cannons. As it grew dark, the English trucks, loaded with their fallen soldiers, drove past our house, and we were struck by the high toll our liberators had to pay for us to regain our freedom.

*

In the aftermath of the war, remnants of human invention and destruction lay scattered around. They fascinated us. In a field, we found four burnt-out Caterpillar vehicles. A heavy-duty German Tiger tank stood in front of one farm with its engine still running and its cannon pointing downwards. Its crew was gone, but there was an ample supply of grenades and even two Schmeisser machine guns. Naturally, we boys couldn't wait to climb inside and pull and turn all the levers and wheels. We were fortunate not to be shot when we moved the turret. British soldiers arrived, dragged us away by our collars and told us in no uncertain terms what a lucky escape we'd had. The crew of an anti-tank cannon had seen the turret turn and thought the Germans were about to open fire. Just in time, the noise of children playing had caused the infantry to intervene.

My friends and I, who had grown up in occupied territory surrounded by weapons and grenades, considered the scattered war materials our toys. The large open-sided Romney sheds were for storing our playthings. British and Canadian soldiers filled them with mortar and cannon grenades, ammo belts, chests with millions of machine gun shells, hand grenades, Bangalore torpedoes, phosphorus shells, dynamite, cargo loads of gunpowder for the cannons and much more.

There was almost no surveillance of the endless rows of open sheds in the fields, so we could take anything that took our fancy. We used a screwdriver to beat or twist the warheads out of the heavy grenade shells and took the gunpowder and detonators home. We used the bullets to fire English Tommy guns and American Thomson machine guns in the woods. The latter were dangerous because the heavy .45 ammo made the weapon jump in our small hands. We caught the empty cases ejected by the machine guns in a bucket so that we could sell or swap them. While exploring ditches or potholes, we often found so-called potato mashers, the hand grenades the Germans had left behind. There was a cap on the wooden handle, and under it was a ring with a cord. Fortunately, we knew from a soldier that we only had six seconds after removing the cord before the thing exploded.

Fons at 12 years old

We filled old petrol jerry cans with gunpowder, set fire to them, closed the lid quickly, and dived into the shelter. The steel cans creaked as they swelled up and exploded after barely five seconds. They flew 30 metres into the air with a thundering bang with their dangerously frayed edges. It was

5

also great fun to light sticks of gunpowder and kick them out, making them surge through the air while they whistled like rockets. Not surprisingly, we called these whistlers. Placing a fuse next to a pile of gunpowder and letting it explode was also a much-loved, ear-shattering activity. Nobody thought to stop us since the racket we made had been a natural element of the surrounding noise landscape for several years. We made sure our parents were unaware of the exact nature of our 'going out to play with friends'.

With Belgium's liberation, the American air defence artillery was active in the neighbourhood. Their assignment was not to let a single German bomb get near the port of Antwerp, and their radar-guided cannons fired relentlessly at the V-1 flying bombs. Sometimes the rapid-fire guns hurled 15,000 glowing 40-millimetre grenades into the air, so it rained metal and was too dangerous to go outside. The schools often closed for weeks.

The bombs flying in London's direction were frequently caught above the English Channel by fighter planes. A V-1 flying bomb with a stalled engine took a perfect glide and landed undamaged in a nearby field. Of course, my friends and I were the first to tinker with the bomb and turn its detonation counter. Shocked British soldiers stopped us just in time and took the object with them to examine it further.

One pitch-dark evening, my father took me outside and told me to lie down and be quiet. A V-1 with a silent engine and with its steering out of control whooshed above our house at a low altitude. It circled and flew over our heads several times, increasingly losing altitude. We lay paralysed with fear until, one minute later, a thundering explosion told us it was all over. Fortunately, it had landed in a field 200 metres up the road and caused minor damage.

At the beginning of 1945, my mother, my sister and I were in our living room when the whole house collapsed around us with an ear-shattering noise. We were surrounded by wooden beams, planks, bricks, and panels, choking on clouds of dust, trying to understand what had happened. It turned out that a V-1 had dropped almost vertically from the sky after being crippled by the air defence and came down only 30 metres from our house. The blast of 725 kilograms of explosives had created a crater nearly eight metres wide. Miraculously, we only had minor injuries.

The war often scared me. Of course it did; our house had been destroyed. And, like everyone, I wanted it to end. But I also found it exciting. Those extensive war experiences toughened me up and gave me a different perspective. I was not afraid of anything and was ready to seek a life full of challenge and often danger. I can confidently say that my childhood was fantastic and filled with endless sunshine, particularly in the aftermath of the war. This positive outlook, unheard of in my little village, became my foundation for building a life brimming with boundless adventure.

*

After a short period, the villagers began to repair the war damage, and we returned to school. Here, our interests were diverted from explosives to other matters: girls. Our teachers insisted on keeping us boys away from the girls, who were guarded by anxious nuns to make sure we wouldn't have a chance to go near them. But after school, my friends and I would meet up with girls in secret. Playing doctors and nurses was a favourite game, and medical treatments always seemed to involve the patients taking off their underwear, even when we only had to cure imaginary earache.

We laughed and rolled carefree from one school year to another. Those who had not studied much before the exam brought the teacher a big fish or another present. Miraculously, the tests always turned out a lot easier after that. The Ministry of Education finally discovered our little village. One day, an inspection commission from the capital came to our school to test our knowledge. We struggled to give sensible answers to any of their questions. One student even enthusiastically proclaimed that Brussels was the capital of France. Unsurprisingly, he was also the one who had brought the most fish for the teacher. When I finally had the chance to speak, I informed them that we had not learnt much because Adolf Hitler had driven us into the shelters for three years. The teacher looked at me gratefully. Later we more than compensated for the backlog, and in the years to come, ingenious thinkers would emerge from our class.

My village was full of ditches covered in duckweed. We would push it aside and drink the water greedily if we were thirsty. A joy lost forever. I would test the floating capabilities of rafts I made from wooden planks and food containers in these ditches and pools. They often failed, and as I couldn't swim, this left me writhing and squirming until I reached the other shore, covered in duckweed. At the time, I did not realise that these early attempts were the beginning of my great ocean adventures in later life.

In my early youth, the village had only two telephones and very few cars. You were seen as a daredevil explorer if you had visited Antwerp, 30 kilometres up the road. When I was 13, two daring students left our village to study at the seminary to become priests. 'God called them,' our teacher announced proudly while the rest of us tried to imagine a world beyond our village. My time came when I reached the age of 14. There was no further education in our village, so if I wanted to acquire more knowledge, I would have to move elsewhere.

By this point, I had been dreaming of navigating the ocean by raft for a long time. My dreams were met with amused dismissal from my parents, but that didn't deter me. In the garden of our house, I set up a makeshift shipyard, repurposing old empty barrels and shaping tree trunks into a floating object. In my youthful ignorance, I was a proud raft builder, unaware that my creation, while fit for a small river, would be blasted to smithereens by the wrath and power of the ocean waves.

As time passed, I recognised I would need to gather the technical knowledge necessary to make my dreams of building unusual seaworthy vessels a reality. So, every day for two years, I sat on a sluggish steam train to attend Antwerp's technical school. The train took an hour and a half to cover the 30-kilometre journey to the port city, and soon I'd had enough of the mundane commuting.

So, instead of regular education, I enrolled in various technical courses, selecting the ones that seemed most relevant to my oceanic endeavours. I started making calculations that would later help me build seaworthy vessels. This conscious decision to step away from mainstream education and focus on my specific interests was something I never regretted. The seed of the thought of crossing an ocean on a raft, planted in my young mind, grew over time. The yearning for adventure and discovery proved irresistible and would eventually shape the rest of my life.

As I started to imagine a life beyond the limits of Nieuwmoer, I joined the Danish pen-pal club and established my first international connections. Before long, I had female pen pals in 20 countries across all the continents. I chose girls, not just out of youthful interest but because I had in the back of my mind the idea that one day I would visit them in their countries and perhaps find someone willing to travel around the world with me.

*

Fons on his motorbike

When I reached the age of 20, I completed my obligatory 18-months military service. The world was calling and I was ready to answer. I put my sleeping bag, cutlery, passport and world map into my backpack and worked up the courage to tell my parents about my plan to hitchhike around the world.

In 1958, I began my long journey thinking it would take two or maybe three years. This was a time untouched by destructive tourism, a time when the chances of meeting other adventurers were low. All alone, on a second-hand, gearless Cyclemaster, I covered the 3,000 kilometres to Istanbul in 30 days. This was a conventional bike with a motor, fuel tank, engine and carburettor built into a wheel and I soon discovered that climbing mountain ranges was too much for its weak, two-stroke, smoking engine, meaning that I had to get off and push. I had some close calls along the way – an encounter with bears in Marshall Tito's old Yugoslavia and a near-fatal shooting in Kavala when local hunters mistook me for a wolf.

My journey also took me through dangerous highways from Zagreb to Belgrade and barren stretches on narrow, dusty back roads all the way to the Greek border. Finally, I arrived in beautiful Greek Thessaloniki, looking like a tired and dishevelled nomad.

After a short stay in Istanbul, I sold my worn out Cyclemaster to a student and continued my journey by public transport, hitchhiking and on foot, always it seemed, heading towards the sunrise in the east. I meandered through Egypt, Lebanon, Saudi Arabia, Iraq, Iran, Afghanistan and Pakistan and on through India to Thailand. One city stood out for me. It was fabled Baghdad, the city of my dreams, where I stayed for two weeks. The violence of war had not yet damaged this beautiful, historic city. It offered a natural and warm Arab hospitality, and I was often invited for a meal as the honoured guest.

Trekking through the Iraqi and Arabian deserts was an early exercise in survival. To travel through the inhospitable terrain I had to join local caravans. The Bedouin traversed the desert outside the established routes using celestial bodies as their guide, which opened my eyes to this ancient means of navigation. We communicated through sign language as they spoke no English and I didn't understand Arabic.

I also travelled through Cairo and Beirut, and it was in these Arab cities that I met the first generation of "Angry Young Men" from Europe and America. My discussions with them did not make us closer, nor did I join them. Unlike them, I was happy, contented and positively charged. I continued my path, which would later become part of the legendary hippie trail to Kathmandu in Nepal, where I encountered messy, hairy men and free-spirited, open-minded girls in flowing skirts. These were the pioneers of the sex-and-drugs generation. Although I identified myself as part of this generation, I felt no connection with their hazy, vague and aimless conversations, fuelled by drug-induced experiences and devoid of deeper meaning.

Instead I sought purpose, and as I travelled I wrote about my experiences. My thirst for adventure and my love of storytelling allowed me to share my experiences with others through various magazines. I wrote not just to touch lives, but to inspire others to break free, explore and live this same kind of incredibly enriching life. Through the highlands of Iran and Afghanistan, I hauled my backpack for weeks on end, losing ten kilograms in weight. I spent nights under the open sky in my little tent, or as a guest in villagers' homes.

When I finally reached the border between Afghanistan and Pakistan, I had to join a military convoy to cross the infamous Khyber Pass, controlled as it was by robbers and thieves. I could not help but be impressed by the knowledge that great conquerors such as Darius I, Alexander the Great and Genghis Khan had crossed this same mountain pass centuries before.

As I travelled through India, I was shocked by the misery and poverty, particularly in Calcutta (now Kolkata). At times, the solitude of the journey became a burden. I sought as much contact with the locals as possible, but I sometimes felt lonely. So, after months of extraordinary encounters and experiences, my travels came to an end in Thailand. A growing longing for companionship and a severe sprain in my leg pushed me to make a difficult decision. Reluctantly, I bid farewell to the open road and boarded a flight home to Belgium. However, the end of that one adventure marked the beginning of countless others; the world was calling and I was eager for the next chapter to unfold.

*

Travelling across the world is no longer a big deal. An aircraft whisks the generally maladjusted tourist to the farthest continent in hours, sadly without letting them experience the countries in between. But, back then, I had adventures that would be impossible in our current world of fast-paced communication and madness. I had the travel bug, and in the following years, I continued my trek by bicycle around Europe and North Africa. Adventure became my profession!

It was during this period, in 1964, that I married one of my Dutch pen pals, Agatha, and we went on to have two children, Ingrid and John. Even though Agatha was not the adventurous type, I enjoyed her company and our travels together. Along with my love of travel, I was also becoming increasingly immersed in technology. My role as a technician involved working with hydraulics, electronics and machine building and it dominated my life. My employment at the time helped fund my own out-

Gyro Captain Fons piloting his gyrocopter

of-hours projects. I built balloons and made 90 flights with them. I also designed and assembled several gyrocopters – one using a Volkswagen Beetle engine - which I flew myself in my spare time, sometimes at the expense of my own safety. Vividly etched in my memory is the moment when the bench I had crafted for rotor blade testing unexpectedly soared skyward, flying an incredible 20 metres into the air. Chaos ensued as the bench took everything with it, crashing back to the ground with a cacophony of shattering components and parts flying everywhere. Another perilous occasion was when I was piloting a prototype helicopter and the rotor blades made contact with the unforgiving concrete runway, instantly shattering the machine. The close brushes with danger were a sobering reminder of the risks involved.

But these experiences were not in vain. They allowed me to hone my technical skills, gaining valuable insights that would prove useful as I prepared myself for future ambitious aeronautical and maritime projects. Through it all, my old and underlying dream of crossing the ocean with a primitive raft never left me and instead became an unstoppable desire.

Dreams Adrift
Atlantis

It was 1973, and I couldn't wait any longer to make my dream come true: crossing the Atlantic on a raft. The route would be 4,300 kilometres from east to west, from the Canary Islands to the American continent, drifting, sailing a little, using the northeasterly trade wind and sea currents to reach our final destination.

My original plan of building a raft from tree trunks was not going to work. There was no suitable wood to be found in Western Europe; not a single species had the buoyancy I required. After an intense search, I discovered a four-metre inflatable raft in the Netherlands made from nylon neoprene. It was a Bombard Besto, the type used in ocean-going commercial shipping as life rafts. Its buoyancy was incredible, but its vulnerability was a disadvantage. It would come down to avoiding sharp objects, and I would need to be careful of any friction. The raft had neither keel nor rudder and even the manufacturer advised me against sailing in it – but I knew it would work out. I built in a multiplex wooden floor on the flexible bottom. This provided a flat and solid base for movement and sleeping on.

It could take three months to reach Trinidad or Barbados from the Canary Islands, although the destination was purely theoretical since there was no way to steer the raft and it might just as well end up in Venezuela. I would have to carry considerable quantities of food and water on board, mainly because I decided to take along a companion. The supplies would need to be canned and dried food, along with army emergency rations. Obviously, cooking was impossible because of the fire risk. We would take on about 100 litres of water in strong plastic bags and would also carry a small desalinisation system that worked on solar heat.

I knew it would be a challenging voyage that would push the crew to the limit. Whether or not someone was suitable would only become apparent once we were out in the deep with no way back.

Eventually, I found Omer, a sporty Antwerpian. Omer was tough. He had been a wrestling champion six times and even participated in the Olympic Games in Melbourne. More importantly, we seemed to agree on things, and he was excited about the voyage.

In the spring of 1974 I contacted the Compagnie Maritime Belge. Their shipping route to the Congo passed the Canary

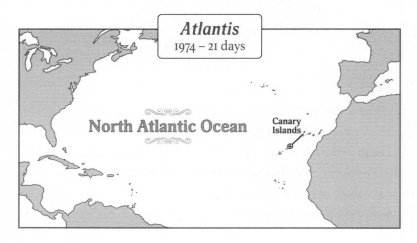

Atlantis
1974 – 21 days

North Atlantic Ocean

Canary Islands

Islands, so I asked if they could drop off the raft on the open seas. They were willing to do so south-west of the small island of El Hierro. This location would place us right in the Atlantic Ocean, limiting any inconvenience from shipping traffic and giving us the benefit of southwesterly currents to take us in the right direction.

Omer and I discussed the enterprise in detail. I had bought the navigation instruments: a Davis sextant, a nautical calendar and the northern Atlantic Ocean's pilot charts. These maps are a treasure trove of information, showing the direction and strengths of currents and winds, as well as hurricane data. I also needed a survival radio transmitter. I bought one of the famous "Gibson Girls" from a trader in second-hand army goods – tiny emergency transponders that were curved in the middle like the shape of a woman's waist.

Our "Gibson Girl" survival radio

Then the time came. Saying goodbye to my wife Agatha and our two children was not easy. After all, it was a dangerous adventure in which all sorts of misfortunes were possible. The dockworkers brought our equipment onboard the *Mobeka*. This cargo ship, under Captain Houard, would need seven days to reach the Canary Islands.

*

It was still dark on 19 May 1974 when the steward woke us up. The entire crew was on deck to watch and help. I had christened my raft *Atlantis*. She slowly swung over the handrail and descended softly onto calm waves. Omer climbed down to receive our equipment while I filmed the event. By the time I descended onto the dancing raft, it was 6am.

We were cast off, and the *Mobeka* slid away behind us. Onboard, the crew raised all flags, and their siren blared. We waved and watched them disappear until, 20 minutes later, the ship was out of sight. The *Mobeka's* chief engineer, who I met years later, told me that none of the crew gave us any chance of surviving.

Even without our small sail, the Canary Current propelled us along. The canopy we'd erected as a shelter caught the trade wind, giving us a little wake. The raft floated impressively, and despite her loaded displacement with the two of us on board, was only submerged about five centimetres, providing more freeboard

Omer onboard Atlantis

than I had expected. We took it in turn to keep watch, switching every two hours. The small hurricane lantern on the short mast didn't give much light. The raft carried herself well on the vast, star-lit, rolling waves. Not a drop of water entered, and the pitch-black night had an eerie feel. I was happy to see the first light of dawn as the warming sun slowly appeared above the horizon, El Hierro's mountain tops visible in the distance.

*

The sunrise also marked a change in the adventure: Omer looked glum and said nothing. The heat became unbearable, even with the canopy to protect us from the scorching sun. I did my best to tidy our tiny bobbing household, which mainly involved shifting supplies and gear around. Omer did not attempt to help. Later that day, just 24 hours after we had been lowered into the ocean, he declared that he'd had enough and wanted to go home. His off-hand remark hit me like a bombshell. Was the beginning of our enterprise about to become the end of it?

Omer begged me to transmit an emergency signal. If he was serious, I would be forced to try to abandon the voyage. The problem was that we were outside the shipping routes with no radio contact.

I couldn't believe that someone who had joined me so enthusiastically would pack it in so soon. My hope that he was suffering from a passing mood turned out to be in vain. Omer continued to beg me to stop. He threatened to jump overboard if I did not pay heed to his request.

Never before had I seen anyone change so dramatically

Being in a very small raft surrounded by high waves terrified him. Under such circumstances, it became impossible for me to continue. Never before had I seen anyone change so dramatically in such a short space of time. He was a different person. I found it unbearable, but I would not let anything happen to him. The life of my companion was my priority. My rafting voyage was something I could attempt again. My dilemma was that we were in an area with almost no traffic, so we had to press on regardless. I held on to the idea that I could continue on my own if we were lucky and could get Omer onto a passing ship. But time was tight as we faced the approaching hurricane season. We were also in an area with almost no traffic. I also held on to the idea that I could continue on my own if we were lucky and could get Omer onto a passing ship. The next day I promised to send out a message on the radio. Whether anyone would hear us was another matter altogether. The receiver required a long wire aerial and the use of a kite or balloon. Over the next few days, we made a lot of attempts to get the kite to fly, but the turbulent air currents made this impossible as the trade wind gathered force. Even without sails, we were covering 20 nautical miles a day.

Whenever a boat appeared, I would shoot a flare to get its attention; but this was rare, because we were now entirely outside any shipping routes, making our way towards the sunset in the west.

My hope that Omer would come to terms with the situation did not work out. As the days passed, he remained apathetic and never once laughed. He remained silent and repeatedly threatened to jump overboard. Omer was terrified of the immensity and loneliness of the ocean and the waves of over four metres that we were encountering. This state of affairs made it unbearable for me too. We continuously scanned the endless ocean. The sun burnt our bodies relentlessly. Omer had been smart enough to keep his shirt on despite the high temperatures. I had defied the sun with my naked upper body but had to pay the price. My skin became so severely burnt that I could hardly lie down to sleep for several days. Plus, the life raft was neither a comfortable nor comforting way to travel. With only flimsy flooring and lacking any kind of superstructure, she was very light and moved with every ripple of the water.

June was already upon us and the hurricane season would soon begin. Even if we were found quickly, any delay would make it impossible for me to continue the voyage alone. Now I knew that it had all been in vain, my attitude changed. The endless desolation began to get under my skin too.

On the ninth day, two large triangular fins appeared above the water: whitetip sharks, three metres long, and very dangerous. They squirmed around the raft, their high fins scraping along the bottom every time they swam underneath and their noses bumping into the side. I was afraid that their rough skin would damage the nylon, so we chased them away using our oars.

*

Our location was now 200 nautical miles south-west of El Hierro. The Canary Current would deflect gradually to the west, which meant that a floating object like ours was unlikely to reach the Cabo Verde islands to the south, no matter how close they were.

The atmosphere onboard remained sombre. Omer would mainly stare into the air and only helped me in efforts related to stopping the voyage. He had confirmed his intention to kill himself if I did not stop and was making recordings of

Fons at sea: The atmosphere onboard remained sombre

his thoughts and intentions on tape and in writing. He did this without any sign of hesitation. I asked him to record this, convinced that there would be trouble if I arrived alone or was found without my companion.

Then something unforgettable happened. From a distance of less than 90 metres, we saw something like the surf of a large wave. A whale suddenly rose out of the water next to our raft. The blue whale was at least 20 metres long and must have weighed 70 tonnes. We could see its beard, which separated plankton from the seawater. The horizontal tail was the width of a living room floor. A feeling of bewilderment overcame us as we watched the impressive, giant, dark cylinder of the greatest being that ever inhabited Earth.

It circled our humble vessel in smaller and smaller rings, and we loosened our little plastic dinghy so that one of us at least would have a rescue vessel if it should destroy our nylon raft. At a distance of 30 metres, the water first became very still, but the sea suddenly came apart as the whale erupted through the surface. With its back above water, it glided towards us fast. Paralysed with fear, we prepared for the worst. A couple of moments before a fatal collision, the whale dropped away and slid under us in an infinite movement before disappearing out of sight.

Just before this encounter, I had determined our location. We had been under way for almost three weeks, and an average speed of 24 kilometres per day had taken us to a point 480 kilometres south-west of the Canary Islands. It was now a certainty that we would never be able to reach Cabo Verde. I thought it better not to tell Omer this.

*

On 9 June, Omer kept watch until midnight when I took over. The stars stood low on the horizon and sometimes disappeared when a massive wave obscured our sight. Coming out of nowhere, I saw two lights a short distance apart. They appeared and disappeared at regular intervals. It was a ship! The lights were west of us, moving in a northerly direction.

We had to act fast to get their attention. The flares! I held one upright in my left hand and pulled the trigger. Four seconds later, the flare shot up, a fierce, red light combusted at 90 metres and a small parachute opened. Nothing happened. The lights continued on their trajectory, and the ship sent no signals. The crew had not spotted the flare. I watched Omer's reaction tensely, afraid that this would have serious consequences. I was also worried about the high risk of firing off flares from the confined space of our nylon raft.

I grabbed a second flare and fired it. The detonator sizzled and exploded after four seconds, but the flash remained in the launch tube. We only had four flares, and if the same thing happened to the third one, we only had one chance left. With a mixture of anticipation and anxiety, we counted the four seconds after firing it. To my immense relief, the flare took off. We strained our eyes, focusing intently on the navigation lights in the distance. Each passing second felt like an eternity until we saw a blinking light on the ship. The crew had spotted our distress signal.

Slowly, the ship came closer, and with the engines off, the captain left the vessel silently drifting towards us. They could not locate us on the radar monitor because nylon and rubber did not reflect the radar beams, so we set off handheld magnesium signals that brightly lit up the outline of the raft until, all of a sudden, we were caught in strong floodlights.

The first thing the crew shouted at us was: 'Where's your ship?' They thought we were survivors of a shipwreck and did not understand what I meant when I said that this was, in fact, our ship. Omer promptly packed his things into a bag while I caught a line thrown to me, which I had to hook onto the raft. A second nylon rope was thrown, which I tied around Omer's waist and under his arms. He was hoisted on board and immediately taken to a bunk. I managed to put my camera and the films into a bag. That and the experience were all I had to show for the journey.

The raft bobbed up and down next to the ship, and at the highest point, I jumped onto the swinging storm ladder and climbed aboard the German ore carrier *Stadt Bremen*. It was quarter to two in the morning, one and a half hours after the freighter had spotted us.

The crew tried to pull *Atlantis* on board, but when she was almost within reach of our hands, the thin ropes broke, and the raft fell back into the sea, landing about ten metres from the ship. Reaching the raft would require long and complicated manoeuvres. Someone had the idea of riddling *Atlantis* with rifle bullets and sinking her. However, the third mate pronounced this impossible because of the raft's many air chambers. The officers convinced me that there was no other option but to leave her where she was. It was heart-wrenching for me, but there it was. At least the raft would not be a danger to shipping. The journey had ended.

The location of *Stadt Bremen* was 23° 08' N 22° 53' W or 380 nautical miles south-west of the Canary Islands. My estimated

MS Stadt Bremen

Günter Platzer | Friends of Seafaring, Emden

positioning on *Atlantis* had been correct. I never heard of the raft again, but it is almost inevitable that it reached the other side of the Atlantic Ocean.

We were welcomed warmly onboard the huge 282-metre bulk carrier. It was a change from the crew's monotonous daily routine, and it was also a good, real-life rescue exercise. *Stadt Bremen* was under Captain Donat's command and was on her way from Brazil to Rotterdam with her cargo of 130,000 tonnes of iron ore.

As soon as we boarded, Omer's behaviour instantly changed. He even blamed me for the failure of our voyage. In fact, the voyage was far from a failure; after three weeks in the ocean, *Atlantis* was still in good shape and had fared well in challenging conditions. Where I clearly had failed was in my pre-journey assessment of Omer's potential as a crew member. My initial impression was overly influenced by his athletic achievements, including his wrestling participation in the 1956 Melbourne Olympic Games. I failed to foresee him collapsing under the pressure of the immense ocean and then asking me to stop just 24 hours after being dropped into the Atlantic. The main problem after that was Omer's inability to recognise that leaving *Atlantis* was easier said than done. Stopping a raft is impossible. The only option was to keep going and hope a ship spotted us.

But we got lucky and he ended up with what he wished for, albeit several weeks after he first demanded that we abandon our voyage. We were also lucky, once safely aboard *Stadt Bremen*, to end up in Rotterdam – just 80 kilometres from Antwerp. The telegram that I had the crew send from the ship never arrived. Agatha was astounded when she opened the front door.

Looking back, I still don't consider this voyage as a failure. *Atlantis* performed superbly and it was an unforgettable adventure. Technically and nautically, the enterprise could be called a success. Where it had fallen short was in the crucial aspect of human behaviour, but those mistakes taught me a lot. For the future, I decided to pay a lot more attention to selecting travelling companions for the crossings I was already contemplating; as it turned out, though, that did not work out quite the way I hoped!

An Ocean Calls

Last Generation, Voyage 1

It was not long after the partial failure of my first raft voyage on board *Atlantis* that I started to prepare for a new Atlantic raft venture. During those days at sea, I'd become fascinated and amazed by the marine life around me, realising the opportunities for study and information gathering as we drifted on winds and currents. I wanted a greater sense of purpose for my next voyage and was keen to focus on research. As I thought about the majestic creatures I'd seen, I couldn't shake my concern for their future. The pollution I'd seen in parts of the ocean felt like an omen of what lay ahead. So, I named my new raft *Last Generation* to acknowledge that, if we continued down this path of environmental neglect, my generation might be the last to witness the ocean's wonders in all their glory. I approached various international bodies seeking support for my plans for research during our voyage. To my surprise and delight the United Nations showed interest and also gave approval for *Last Generation* to fly the UN flag.

I wanted more space onboard this time, and a stable deck, so I decided to build a raft from pipes. In Antwerp's port, I discovered a stack of rusty dredging pipes, six metres long and with a diameter of 70 centimetres. That was all I needed to build a primitive but stable floating vessel. I called the owner and was happy to hear that I could collect seven pipes free of charge.

My smallholding now became a shipyard. As soon as I had the design and construction plan on paper, I got down to work. I designed the raft with a beam of nearly five metres and an overall length

Raft pipes in the yard

of eight metres. Four of the pipes formed the main base of the raft in a quadrimaran structure. I then attached two V-shaped pipe sections onto the front end to serve as the raft's double prow. These were securely bolted in place. To ensure stability and strength, the pipes forming the four hull sections were firmly joined together by cross beams. The pipes themselves would serve as dry cargo space and as reservoirs for drinking water.

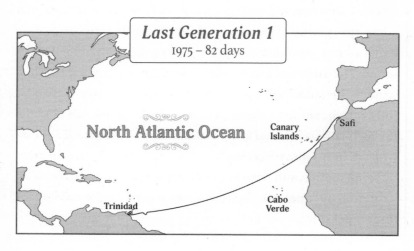

Last Generation 1
1975 – 82 days

North Atlantic Ocean

Canary Islands

Safi

Trinidad

Cabo Verde

Given what had happened with Omer, I thought I'd be better with a crew of three this time. Raoul De Boel from Ghent replied to my advert. He had seafaring experience as a carpenter on a freighter and was the first to sign up. I insisted that he work with me on constructing the raft, realising his practical skills would be useful and also that this would give us a chance to get to know each other before setting sail. During my previous undertakings, I'd experienced feelings of isolation; so I wanted to have radio contact this time. An amateur radio enthusiast helped me obtain a short-wave transceiver.

Raoul and I made good progress. We cut a big tree into planks and mounted these onto supports. We made a double V-shaped mast from two eight-metre pipes, each ten centimetres in diameter. The legs were two metres apart and placed on universal joints, enabling movement in every direction. The yard that the square sail was attached to was a round pipe. I welded a ring onto both ends to brace the sail, which was essential for navigation and keeping on course since, without a sail, all the vessel could do was drift on the currents.

In the middle of the decked raft, we placed a two-metre-square cabin covered with robust, dark green canvas, in which I had two plastic windows specially made. Because the trade wind would predominantly be coming from the north-east, we put the entrance on the port side, away from the prevailing wind. In lieu of a fixed keel, we constructed and fitted leeboards for steering. Sliding rails welded onto each corner would allow the leeboards, each one and a half metres long and half a metre wide, to move up and down. The sail was five and a half metres by seven metres, and I made it from the same canvas as the cabin – durable material used by the military to make the roofing for army trucks.

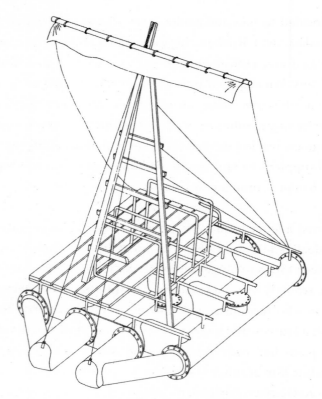

Drawing of raft Last Generation

Throughout the construction phase I contacted people who might offer guidance. I asked for advice from a retired sea captain, who told me that my raft would never make an ocean crossing. Fortunately, his wife was able to give me a more useful tip: she mentioned that a French bulk cargo ship, *Pengall,* regularly sailed from Antwerp to Safi in Morocco. I followed up with my contact in the shipping company and soon received the offer that *Pengall* would provide free passage for the raft and crew to the African coast.

We next visited a doctor for medical advice and took home stacks of antibiotics, bandages and even surgical scalpels. I also decided to take 100 Kodachrome II 16mm film cassettes. Filmmaker Wim Robberechts provided a handy, shockproof 16mm Bell and Howel camera and an excellent 10mm wide-angle lens. We acquired pre-cooked meals in tins, along with nutritious biscuits, oatmeal, macaroni, milk powder, brown and white sugar, butter, corn oil and canned meat, 50 kilograms of potatoes, bottled drinks, and sweets such as chocolate. We would supplement our provisions in Morocco with subtropical fruits, bananas, oranges and olives.

*

I received a letter from a Moroccan named Hassan Chribatou, who declared himself to be in good health and willing to volunteer for the voyage without pay. The same captain who had so strongly advised me against attempting the crossing was the one who recommended Hassan to me. It was only much later that I discovered he only did so to escape Hassan's nagging; the captain had once promised him work, and Hassan kept reminding him of this.

On 10 October, *Pengall* left Antwerp in the pouring rain. My wife, Agatha, always put on a brave face, and this send-off was no different. Our children, Ingrid, 11, and John, 9, found it all very interesting. Besides Raoul and Hassan, my wife was the only one with any faith in the endeavour. She had even taken a job as a night nurse to earn more money, and she faced all the challenges my absence brought. Few wives would be prepared to do what she did.

It took five days for *Pengall* to take us to Morocco, and in mid-October, we moored at Safi, where we met Hassan. He kissed and hugged us. *Last Generation* was unloaded, and we slowly guided the three-tonne raft through the four-metre opening in the rail. The winch drum slowly lowered the pipes downwards to enter the water for the first time. The raft lay perfectly horizontal in the crystal-clear harbour water.

That evening we were the captain's guests. Among the other guests was a man who praised Hassan's knowledge of coastal navigation but warned us about his temperamental character. That came as a shock to me, but I did not see it as a direct reason not to take him with us. Later, I would come to wish I'd paid more attention to this warning.

We dragged the raft to a quieter spot, away from the noisy phosphate loading area, so we could work more comfortably and not get coated in white dust. Hassan and I made our way to the shipyard to have the leeboards made. The planks for this had to be as strong as iron and in one piece, and we needed wood for the floor of the cabin.

I also bought two hurricane lanterns, a foghorn and clevis hooks that we could use to hook ourselves to the raft in the event of a storm. The next day, we took the rudder to a smithy to have a tiller welded onto it. The rudder had sturdy hinge pins, four centimetres thick, making it unlikely to break. Hassan attached the small compass table to the deck using a thick rope. I had a small but excellent army compass that I wouldn't dream of trading for a more modern one.

I enjoyed the days of preparation. I could smell the ocean air and feel the already familiar raft underfoot as I looked forward to the challenge ahead. One crucial task was to procure a life raft before we set sail. However, despite numerous attempts, we soon realised that there were no inflatables to be had in Safi. As an alternative, we considered using one of the rigid rescue boats favoured by local fishermen but they were too heavy and cumbersome to carry. Left with no other option, we had to place all our faith in our raft.

*

26 October, Raoul and I were up early. Hassan arrived soon afterwards. A fishing boat would tow us out to sea at 9am. Luckily, the wind came from the north-east, ideal for us to leave the African coast. We raised the flags of the United Nations, Morocco and Belgium. Some men on the pier shouted to Hassan that he was crazy but, encouragingly, he did not show any signs of being affected.

At 10.45am, the moment I had dreamed of arrived. The ship's engine revved, and *Last Generation* jolted as the towing line tightened. A feeling of relief surged in me now that the long, sometimes cumbersome preparations were behind us. I felt the freedom ahead of me and was happy that we would soon be alone in the ocean. But first we had to be towed at least five miles offshore to ensure that despite the favourable wind, the moody turbulent currents would not push the raft back onto land. A force 3 was blowing, and the bright sun shimmered in the Atlantic, gradually changing its hue.

By around 3.30pm, the raft was far enough from the coast to potentially catch currents that could help us. We hoisted the sail so the raft could get onto her course of 230°. The wind was north-by-north-east and made the canvas bulge. Soon, there was nothing but sea surrounding us.

I intended to steer as far in a westerly direction as possible to distance us from the coast. Sailing due west was impossible because the current propelled us south. We braced the sail as much as possible using the rudder and stayed on course. After experimentation, I discovered that the leeboards did most of our steering. Pushing a board 20 centimetres up or down was enough to change course. Slowly the north-east trade wind gathered force, and the raft drifted magnificently over the waves. The water splashed on all sides but did not wash over the deck.

It was essential to have one of us constantly on watch, not only to steer but also because of the risk of collisions with other ships while we were close to the coast. Hassan's watch would be from seven to eleven, Raoul's from eleven to three and mine from three to seven, after which Hassan would take over again. The nightly trade wind at 32° northern latitude was cold. It seemed that we were being propelled faster and faster. We drew a wide trail of light in the foaming water, the phosphorescence clearly visible in the dark. The cross beams groaned and creaked from stress but the raft remained stable. The tanks at the stern provided ballast with 550 litres of water.

Raoul served breakfast in the morning; it turned out that Hassan's culinary skills were non-existent and mine left a lot to be desired. Plus, I was too busy with tasks onboard. Raoul was a bachelor and had acquired some gastronomic experience, so the best solution was to pronounce him the chef of the raft. He was pleased with the title.

When we saw Morocco's mountains in the distance, Hassan pointed to three peaks he recognised. He could not, however, pinpoint where we were on the map. He explained that local fishermen only knew how to navigate along the Moroccan coast at night, and they did it with a Michelin road map. Interpretation was straight forward: many lights on the coastline meant a large town, and few lights meant a small village.

With the land still in sight, we encountered our first setback. The rudder stopped working and the raft drifted off course. It turned out that the joint where the tiller was welded to the rudder had broken. I saw that it had been welded badly in the workshop in Safi. There had been no way of seeing that from the outside.

This was terrible luck, given that we needed the rudder more than ever because of our proximity to Cape Juby. The sail soon began to slacken and flap, so we had no choice but to take it down. We bobbed along, rudderless, at the mercy of the current. I had to find a solution fast. I should be able to fix it using the pipes and spare ropes we had on board. I needed a tube about two metres long. Hassan showed his skills and wound a thick rope crosswise around the tiller, the pipe and the rudder, and we became stable again.

Our next worrying situation emerged several days later when Hassan asked me if we were finally about to reach the other side of the ocean. He felt that it was taking us too long! After my experiences with Omer, I realised immediately that this meant trouble. We had only been on our way for a few days, and I expected it to be another 90 days before we saw land again. As it turned out, Hassan had only ever fished for sardines off the Moroccan coast and had never been at sea for longer than a day. Back in Safi, when I told him that the journey could take more than three months, he had been enthusiastic and said that was no problem. I now realised that he had no concept of time. This was the start of a series of psychological challenges we had to tackle.

From 3am to 7am, my watch provided the unforgettable spectacle of the birth of a new day, when the orange-coloured sun slowly appeared above the horizon. Colours danced across the water's surface while whimsically shaped clouds spread a red glow. Then Hassan took the helm, and I crawled onto my mat exhausted and slept like a dog.

When I woke up, still tired, around 10am, Raoul told me that our portside leeboard had disappeared. We had four boards, so losing one was not a catastrophe, but losing a second one would make it difficult to steer. We kept an eye on the crucial boards from that moment on, tying them down with rope. We had to be able to steer now, as we were at the most dangerous stage of our passage from Safi, south of Casablanca, to Cape Juby in southern Morocco, parallel with the Canary Islands.

One beautiful night when it was completely quiet, we heard the sound of heavy diesel engines in the distance. Shortly afterwards, we saw navigation lights approaching. Hassan begged me to fire a distress flare to get ourselves towed. I disagreed with forcing a large cargo ship to assist us without serious cause. We lay on a calm sea in a seaworthy raft full of food and drinking water. The 48 miles that now separated us from the coast were more than enough to keep us out of the danger zone. That night, Hassan woke me twice more, asking to fire the distress flares. To prevent him from doing so, I slept using the flare box as my pillow.

That afternoon, we made out the giant mountain ranges of the rocky island of Fuerteventura among the clouds. The forceful, turbulent sea currents propelled our raft through the strait, and there before us lay the endless ocean. I felt happy and free; I had adjusted to the sea and was in harmony with the water. Now I could draw a straight line on the map to Cabo Verde. It had taken us ten days to complete the passage from Safi to Cape Juby and from here the Canary Current and north-east trade wind would take us further from the African coast.

We saw a fishing boat the following day. The crew saw us too and turned around to see what strange phenomenon was drifting around out here. It was a chance to ask for some fresh food. We bobbed 15 metres apart on the calm sea as a sailor placed long, golden sticks of bread into plastic bags. They tied these to a thin line which they threw across to the raft and we tied it to the mast. We hauled it in slowly, letting the loaves of bread glide through the air towards us. They were crisp and fresh and very inviting.

The fishermen gestured to us to send the line back again. This time they attached three bottles of Spanish wine. A welcome gift!

We were curious to see what would come next. When we opened the third parcel, we found frozen fish. I had to laugh. The whole operation had taken all of 20 minutes. The diesel engine was revved up again, and the ship set her course in a northerly direction. We waved to each other for a long time. Our kitchen mate Raoul rubbed his hands in glee. That evening, fresh bread, fried fish and wine left us in high spirits, convinced we could rule the waves. We told each other tall tales and shook with laughter. In the meantime, the small, cramped, rolling world that held us drifted on the open ocean under a red sunset that set the western sky on fire. All was well on board *Last Generation.*

Last Generation *Voyage I*

Troubled Waters

Last Generation, Voyage 1

Our good fortune didn't last long. After our radio contact the next afternoon, Hassan flew into a rage and started cursing at me. I didn't understand what was going on. After a lot of back and forth, he claimed that he had heard his name mentioned in the radio conversation and that I'd told people he was sick – even though he did not understand a word of the Dutch or English languages in which the discussions took place. I began to understand. Hassan was very proud and did not want anyone in Safi to know anything was wrong with him. He even suggested that, if he became seriously sick, we should not call any ships but just throw him overboard if he died. This incident spoilt the atmosphere, but we tried to forget it since it was essential to work as a team.

In the afternoon, I was sitting in the cabin, organising our navigation equipment, when I heard Raoul and Hassan shout. I rushed outside. Hassan pointed to something floating close by: a corpse, with its head bobbing up and down on the swell of the sea. We tried to pull the body closer with a pole and rope, hoping to find a way to identify her if possible. It didn't work. The woman's long blond hair vanished behind us as her body slipped away. This disturbing encounter reminded us that life and death are never far apart at sea.

That day, I used the spare yellow sail sitting aimlessly in the storage pipes to increase our speed. We made a five-metre-long yard using a metal tube, which we attached behind the mast, and lay the attached sail across the cabin, producing a big pocket to catch the trade winds. The following day's navigation showed we had covered five miles more in 24 hours. Slowly, the Canary Current changed into the warm Northern Equatorial Current that would take us to the American continent.

*

14 November marked the beginning of a miraculous fishing spree. At least 50 dorados splashed around the raft. I told Hassan we wanted a fish on our plate, whatever it took, and I would catch it myself if necessary. As a fisherman, that touched his pride. He prepared a line with artificial bait and pulled in a spectacular dorado in no time. Having got the hang of it, he put a piece of fish on the treble hook and cast it far behind the raft. The dorado shot towards the bait like a torpedo. Three others followed in its wake. The first one took the bait without hesitation, and it was stuck. Getting it on board was another task as dorados are large, muscly fish. This specimen was only a little smaller than Hassan himself.

23° 22' N, 18° 42' W. The next day, around 2pm, the silhouette of a boat appeared in the distance. We assumed it was a fishing boat, but it turned out to be a cargo ship. They spotted us, adjusted their course, and the *Hungaria* soon lay swaying beside us. They asked us where we were going. Our answer, 'Trinidad,' surprised them. The chief officer used a ship's horn to ask in English if we needed anything. I asked if we could have some bread. The man disappeared and a plastic bag was lowered into the water. We pulled it towards us and, to our delight, found bread, sardines in oil, fruit, three bottles of wine and apple puree inside. We expressed our gratitude, and the *Hungaria* slid away. As if that wasn't enough of a gift, the wind gathered intensity, and with the help of the yellow spare sail, we dashed through the water. That evening, Raoul prepared a delicious meal, which we washed down with a glass of Hungarian wine.

We had been on the Atlantic for three weeks. Life on board wasn't easy. We had to be alert, watching out for dangers day and night. Every day, even though I couldn't swim, I dived into the water wearing flippers with a rope tied around me or let myself be pulled along behind the raft by the 30-metre-long safety rope. Raoul and Hassan never went swimming as they were afraid of sharks. There were not many to be seen, but they could appear at any time.

*

There hadn't been time to treat the raft with anti-fouling to prevent the growth of marine fauna and flora and it began to show. At first, we could just see a bit of green on the pipes. Then barnacles started growing, many reaching lengths of eight centimetres, which disturbed our streamline and slowed us down. Cleaning them off became a regular activity, although scrubbing the raft's underside was practically impossible because we could not stay underwater for long and sharks started to show an interest in what we were doing.

One day Raoul made French fries. It was a strange scene: chips on a raft in a distant ocean. Hassan did not like them. He was fussy about his food. Too weird, too cold, too warm, too fatty, too big, too small. At first, this drove Raoul crazy, until he decided Hassan would have to eat whatever was served or go without his meal. Hassan was frequently unhappy and could often be found staring at a photo of his children. Raoul remained quiet but optimistic. My motivation was also low at times. Food was one thing that could change our moods. Raoul and Hassan maintained their weight, but I noticed I was getting thinner. I was happy to continue losing weight because I felt much healthier than on land.

In the mornings, we often found flying fish on the deck. Attempting to elude the greedy dorados, these fish skimmed the sea about half a metre above the surface. At night, they couldn't see the raft and would crash into the cabin or hit the helmsman, who would then scramble to catch them. Even on rough seas, we often found fish on deck. As the tail of the raft was thrust upwards, the tubes would lift out of the water, and when the raft descended back, the sea would rush over the boards in bubbling, seething waves. Although the cracks in the deck greedily swallowed the abundant water, they sometimes held back a writhing fish.

One morning, we noticed to our surprise that the raft was covered in white dust, although we were almost 485 nautical miles from the coast. At first, we were unsure what was going on, but the only explanation was that the north-east trade wind had brought sand from Africa.

*

26 November. We had been travelling for one month. The distance we had covered was approximately 1,380 miles – more since we had sailed zigzag routes. The day began with a sunrise that tinted the sea in glorious colours. It was 6.30am and my watch was almost over. I suddenly saw what appeared to be stationary, cloud-like formations on the south-east horizon. Could that be land? Ten minutes later, it was visible: the Cabo Verde island of Santo Antão. The highest mountain on the

island was almost 2,000 metres (Tope de Coroa), so it would be visible for some time to come. I decided not to wake Raoul, and let Hassan take over from me and discover the spectacle for himself. When he did, he was wildly enthusiastic and had to admit that my navigational skills, which he had doubted, were not so bad after all.

We came through the second part of the crossing between the Canary and Cabo Verde islands beautifully. However, a lot had happened on this route, including Hassan's dramatic change in behaviour. He was always next to me during the radio broadcasts, listening in case anyone used his name. If his name crackled through the loudspeakers, we risked another fit of anger. He repeatedly asked Raoul if anything had been said about him.

I was tense as I carried out my astronomical observations. The result of my calculations was disappointing. Although we had progressed towards the south, we had only covered 14 miles westward. The southern currents must have been holding us back. We would have to steer a course of 280° to escape their clutches. The weather meant we did not meet my expectations of reaching halfway within a few days. We still had 270 miles to go before reaching longitude 31 west.

At this point, we also realised that the dorados had bitten through all our fishing lines and had gone off with our hooks. We had to improvise. Hassan attached the steel handle of a plastic bucket to a pole to replace the hook, and I dug up a grinding stone to sharpen the hook. As a result, a few mahi-mahi were soon writhing on the deck and Raoul could live out his gastronomic dreams again.

We saw a lot of 'Man O Wars' on our travels. These are jellyfish, also known as 'Portuguese warships' because a small sail sticks out of the water and they use it to move across the sea.

The metre-long tentacles can grow up to ten metres and are very venomous. To neutralise the venom, you can rub ammonia into your body, so we had nine litres on board.

*

Things started looking up on 29 November, when we discovered we were 82 miles west of Cabo Verde – an excellent position. I drew the course line on a map from Santo Antão to Trinidad, our hypothetical destination.

We had been at sea for weeks, and I found my spirits rejuvenated by the healing effect of isolation: no cars, no noise, no dust, and no complaints about unimportant issues to deal with. Raoul laughed and said the lack of women was also an advantage. I took pleasure in walking around the raft, listening to the wind whistle between the stays. I had become surprisingly attached to this floating refuge. We often sat or lay on the cabin floor, mindful of the amoral world that existed beyond our raft – where 'kill or be killed' was a given. Yet, beneath our deck was 4,000 metres of water, in which eternal darkness and silence reigned. Our raft was our only world, and in a primitive vessel like this, we felt an extreme connection to the sea.

*

We were 486 miles west of Cabo Verde and we had a lot of work to do. Five minutes into Hassan's shift, he let the raft move to course 290°. The abrupt shift caused the sail to flap violently and, with a loud bang, one of the sail's sheets was ripped away. Around noon, the tiller broke off again. We were now out of control, and the raft began to spin. The sail had to be taken down to avoid it breaking as it beat against the mast.

I climbed up the mast to cut the rope with a knife. Too late. The sail was now hanging lengthways, so that the wind blew with enormous power into the 38.5-metre-square canvas and the pressure came sideways onto the raft. We tilted over so far that I feared we would capsize, but the raft remained sturdy. Desperate, I kept working on the rope with the knife until it finally broke. I used my body weight to bring down the yard with the flapping sail. It did not work; a rope was still stuck somewhere. I sent Hassan up with a knife, but he lost his grip and dropped it into the waves. I tried to hold back the massive canvas, but it was useless. A loud crack announced that the sail was tearing underneath. But when the halyard finally came loose, the pipe with the sail was lying alongside the raft. Suddenly everything was calm again. We soon restored the rudder and sail, and our raft resumed her course, leaving a gentle wake trailing behind us once again.

More and more sharks were beginning to appear, some of them strikingly beautiful. With its strange shape, the hammerhead shark is probably the most remarkable of all. We saw the man-eater pop up next to us several times. We had an escort of dangerous whitetip sharks swimming with the raft at one stage. That was a fantastic sight.

Raoul continued to work miracles with the limited ingredients available and produced three edible and nourishing meals a day. He regularly sat rummaging through the stocks in our storage cabinet, hoping we would make it to Trinidad before we ran out of things to eat.

The sextant showed we were 81 nautical miles south of our planned course towards Trinidad's north coast. Since losing sight of Cabo Verde, we had covered 730 miles as the crow flies – not bad. We were midway between the African and American continents. The water was 5,180 metres deep.

That afternoon a small freighter approached. The ship was struggling and rocking severely in the waves. We realised why when we came closer. *Inagua Gull,* steaming to West Africa, was top-heavy with three enormous diesel locomotives on deck. We used the chance to ask for water as our supplies were running low. The jolly crew members fished out the two plastic jerrycans, which we tied to the end of our safety line. They threw back the filled containers and we struggled to reel them in to the raft. The battered and rusting coaster then hooted farewell and headed eastwards. We saw the ship swaying in the struggle against the Atlantic waves for a long time before she disappeared.

At times, there was lightning and thunder for a whole day or night; fiery snakes squirmed across the sky and deafening bangs tore into the silence. The welcome rain washed the raft and crew clean, but the water was so cold it made us shiver. Sometimes the rain fell hard enough to enter under the canvas, soaking our sleeping bags. On top of the cabin canvas, a pool of water formed, which we collected in a bucket and used as drinking water.

The next day, during our radio communication, I spoke to Agatha. Feeling optimistic we would eventually reach our planned destination, I asked her to bring clothes and shoes to Trinidad, since my new trousers had disappeared in Safi and I had given Hassan my shoes since he had accidentally dropped his into the water. The rest of my clothes were torn or had blown off the raft into the sea.

I hoped we would land in Trinidad and not keep drifting in the Sargasso Sea. We joked about it, especially when Hassan predicted we would be on land in time for Christmas. Every day I showed him the red line on the map that represented our progress over the last 24 hours. The track already meandered past the 40th longitude. Trinidad is at 61° west, meaning we still had just over 1,600 nautical miles in front of us. Anything could happen.

And it did.

One night, the sail suddenly slatted, flapping angrily. How was that possible with an easterly wind? I put on my windbreaker and leapt out of the cabin. To my surprise, Hassan wasn't at the helm. Fearing he'd fallen overboard, I called for Raoul and turned on the torch we always kept on the navigation table. As we shone the light over the water and the raft, the spare sail on the deck seemed to bulge; our helmsman was fast asleep underneath it. I had to shake him to wake him up, but he insisted that he had never been asleep. I had a suspicion that this was the secret behind our zigzagging route, the way we had drifted south, and even the strangely limited distance we had covered. After that, I no longer trusted Hassan at the helm.

From 18 December to 2 January, we made our fastest progress, averaging 40 nautical miles a day. We were due to pass the shipping route from New York to the east coast of South America. Probably not a busy route, but there was still a chance we would see a ship and once again be able to ask for some water, because this time our situation was becoming desperate. We could only drink half a litre each per day. This was enough to keep our bodily functions going but was becoming torturous and hazardous under the tropical sun. Raoul rationed the biscuits to six per day. We had no potatoes but there were still a few precious cans of food left, including some with apple puree, although he preferred to save those. The distance to Trinidad was another 770 nautical miles. Even if we covered 54 miles every 24 hours, it would take us two weeks to arrive there. Suriname, the closest land, was, for us, now unreachable and 405 miles south-west of our location.

*

By New Year's Day, we were heading due west on a latitude of 11° 19' N. If we could maintain this we would end up between Tobago and Trinidad, meaning we'd only need to be towed a short way to Port of Spain. I estimated we had 513 miles to run to our presumed point of arrival. Over the radio, we received greetings from Raoul's family, my wife, and the rest of my family. I thought about all the people worldwide who were now visiting each other, offering drinks or a glass of beer while we had to make do with our ration of warm, rusty water.

I did not know that the modest distance we covered on the second day of the new year would mark the beginning of the most challenging part of the journey. On the following day, the misery truly commenced. I noticed that we had dropped more than 22 minutes of latitude to 10° 57' N. That was 22 nautical miles, and the sextant did not lie. We were in a westerly current, so in theory we shouldn't be able to drop to lower latitudes. I did not understand it; all we could do was wait. Any hope of landing in Trinidad evaporated.

Five days into the new year, we had been underway for a full 70 days. The previous fortnight had turned out to be the most difficult, particularly for Hassan – and therefore by extension for all of us. The length of the journey, the lack of cigarettes, his inability to read or write or understand radio messages, and a very different mentality had caused him to break down. Raoul and I did everything we could to cheer him up, but it was not easy.

Even worse, we were in the grip of a current, continually drifting south. We were 378 miles from Trinidad and 270 from Suriname. If everything went well, our arrival in South America would be at the end of the next week. All we could do was hope the Southerly Equatorial stream would propel us to higher latitudes. These were tough days for us. The uncertainty, the lousy weather, the food rationing, the poor drinking water, and the psychological pressure took their toll. But I reflected that this was a challenging undertaking, after all, and not a pleasure trip.

*

It was evening and Raoul was due to take over Hassan's watch when the stormy weather suddenly caused the raft to change course. We were out of control. Quickly, I investigated and shone a torch at the place where the starboard leeboard should be. It was gone! Here we were, with just one board left. There was no way to steer the raft, and we were at the mercy of the elements. We urgently needed a solution. The best option was to take planks from the deck to make a new leeboard. I pulled the small generator out and turned on a 100-watt bulb, so a quivering light drove out the darkness. Removing the decking planks was difficult since the bolts that had spent a lot of time submerged in seawater were stuck with rust.

Without warning, I stepped onto a place where one of the planks had been. I fell headlong into the sea. The raft moved on, and I was swallowed up by the night. Frantically, I struggled towards the pipes, wishing I could swim properly. But however hard I worked, the raft propelled the water up and pushed me away. I was lost, but instead of panic or fear, I found myself curious what my end would be like and what would happen afterwards.

Raoul roared, 'The rope. The rope!'

We always dragged our rescue rope behind the raft so that anyone who fell overboard had a chance to grab and hold on to it, but I struggled to find it in the dark with the water as black as ink. Fortunately, Hassan had the inspiration to throw the sea anchor overboard on a ten-metre-long rope. After summoning up a couple of desperate strokes, I caught it at the last moment and pulled myself up. Grasping the rudder with a sigh of relief, I clambered on board. Raoul was in quite a state, but Hassan showed no signs of distress.

One minute later, we saw whitetip sharks, which had come to see what all the splashing and noise were about.

Breathing heavily, we continued with the repairs. With difficulty, we drilled holes in the planks and screwed them together. We lowered the whole thing into the frame and tied it down with strings. It worked beautifully, and once again, we were able to steer.

Several days later, Hassan brought up my fall again. Matter-of-factly, he declared that he would not have liked to see me disappear into the waves because of the trouble he and Raoul would have with the police upon reaching land. This, he explained, was why he had thrown out the sea anchor. I was disconcerted by the revelation!

*

On 8 January, I felt our course changing drastically. We were now drifting in a northerly direction at high speed. We had been 324 miles from Trinidad and 238 miles from Suriname. The next day, we discovered that in 24 hours, we had progressed 25 miles to the west. The currents were so strong here that we would probably end up in Galleons Passage, the 19-mile-wide channel between Trinidad and the small island of Tobago. We discussed a potential landing point, and it looked like we were rushing towards Barbados, St. Lucia, or Martinique. These places were just as suitable as Trinidad for ending our expedition. The main thing was that we would reach the other side of the Atlantic Ocean, alive and well.

The clean air and the ascetic life were healing. The ability, lost to modern man, of subconsciously sensing approaching danger had come back to us. All our primal instincts were alive. We were prepared to react or fight at any moment. The blood rushed through my veins, and I was happy to be there. I had come to appreciate life more as I experienced the abundance of a simple life. Like Raoul, I also found the absence of women to be an advantage, but of course, that was only temporary.

The stark simplicity of our existence was underscored when Raoul announced that we had run out of food. We would have to get by on whatever fish we could catch. Each day, we filled a plastic canister with water, carefully siphoning it from our large container. We had no more cigarettes left. Strangely enough, I found cigarettes more important than edible goods as they could calm Hassan. Raoul, who had smoked with moderation during the trip, did not mind going without. Since we were now so close to the coastline, chances were that a fishing boat would come along and we could ask for some cigarettes.

On Monday 13 January, we looked longingly for an aeroplane that might be scouting for us, but there was not a single aircraft to be seen. I carried out the astronomic navigation and was perplexed but pleased to note that we had covered a considerable distance. The powerful but invisible Southern Equatorial Current had brought us within 81 miles of Trinidad. However, we were also just 60 miles from the dangerous Orinoco Delta in Venezuela and, on top of that, we were in the shallow blue zone, meaning that the situation could become critical.

That night, we saw the navigation lights of fishing boats, and from then on, we powered the generator to light up our own mast-top 100-watt bulb. In the morning we noticed the colour of the seawater changing. Now we were in shallow waters, it was no longer clear.

Our faithful companions, the dorados who had accompanied us for thousands of miles across the ocean, left us, having entertained and fed us. It was announced over the radio that a light aircraft would come looking for us at 2pm and would drop plastic bags with food.

Matthieu, a Belgian ham radio operator, notified us that an aircraft with our friendly cameraman, Wim, and a journalist named Justin had left Port of Spain and would be looking for us at the transmitted position. Around 4pm, a Cessna brushed past, almost touching us. We were found! I was living on adrenaline and was on high alert. The whole night we kept watch together and took turns to sleep for a while.

The next day the Cessna returned and its pilot made a skilful food drop. We retrieved three of the four bags dropped. That night we entered the strait between Venezuela and Trinidad, which was at most 30 metres deep. Thereafter, things became a lot more hazardous for the raft as the channel narrowed like a funnel to just eight miles at Columbus Point, otherwise known by the more apt and sinister name of Serpent's Mouth. We were in danger of strong currents running us onto the Venezuelan shore.

Raoul, sitting in the crow's nest, shouted that something was moving parallel to the raft: a fast coastguard boat. I fired a light flare and threw a smoke signal into the sea, which caused a bright red cloud to appear above the water. Hassan and Raoul were still sitting on the mast, waving wildly. The journey had almost reached its end!

The coastguard heaved to, and we exchanged greetings. The sailors threw us a line, which we attached to the raft. The yacht *Rosita* appeared in the distance. As she came closer, I spotted my wife, Agatha, among the passengers. The *Rosita* circled the raft, and everyone was waving. Together we continued to the southwesterly point of Trinidad. The raft danced behind the coastguard boat, as they dragged us through the water with roaring engines.

Suddenly, our raft lost speed. The line dragging us had broken and slammed against the coastguard boat's stern, becoming tangled in the twin propellers. The sailors hung fenders along the side to prevent a collision, as the captain dived into the water with a knife between his teeth to cut the rope loose. After a little more than an hour, the job was done.

We arrived at Icacos Point at dusk and anchored next to the coastguard and the *Rosita*. We were allowed onboard the yacht, where I could finally hug my wife after being apart for over three months. The journey had ended, and we were all happy to be able to speak to other people again.

The following day, the coastguard continued to tow us and we rounded the Point into the Gulf of Paria and headed towards Port of Spain. We dropped anchor in the marina, and for the first time in 82 days, we set foot on land. For our first few steps, we had trouble finding our balance. Hassan had put on his good suit and Raoul some neat clothes, but I only had my swimming trunks and a rain jacket.

Wistfully, I looked across at the empty raft bobbing softly in the trade wind. What an accomplishment!

Defying Doubts

Last Generation, Voyage 2

My successful Atlantic crossing gave me valuable insights into ocean life and led to many invitations to do lectures about my expeditions. I gave over a thousand lectures in just as many locations in the years that followed, and the enthusiasm I received from my audiences further strengthened my determination to continue. I felt driven by the need to succeed in my experiments and expeditions, and everything else fell into their shadow. I had not yet realised this attitude could often be unpleasant for others. Between my *Atlantis* and *Last Generation* lectures, my full-time job and my work on new vessels for future adventures, I hardly had time for my family. This started to bother my wife, Agatha, who longed for a quieter life.

For some time, I had been preoccupied with the idea of constructing a small submarine-like vessel to take me to the bottom of the North Sea in search of submerged wrecks. But there were many challenges involved in submarine design and construction. On top of that, the marine life I'd encountered during my two raft expeditions had left me more interested in experiencing the underwater world than merely descending 90 metres or so to the North Sea floor to probe the seabed for wreckage. So, I adapted my thinking and came up with a compromise: my next generation vessel, *SeaLab*, which was conceived as a floating laboratory with underwater viewing capabilities. However, *SeaLab* faced its own set of problems during testing, prompting a further evolution in my designs into the more practical vessel that I named *Seaview*. The creation of this boat became an obsession, consuming the majority of my free time.

Sadly, over the next few years, my marriage deteriorated beyond repair. Agatha had been asking how I felt about divorce for quite some time, wanting to walk her peaceful path while giving me the freedom to pursue my own passions. We bore no resentment or regret; our lives had simply drifted in different directions.

So, there I sat, alone on my rustic little farm, determined to remain single for a while, to prevent any romantic entanglements from disrupting my plans. Artists and adventurers share a problem: we often experience unconventional, turbulent and unpredictable relationships.

However, during my presentations about my raft journeys, I often found myself getting into debates with audience

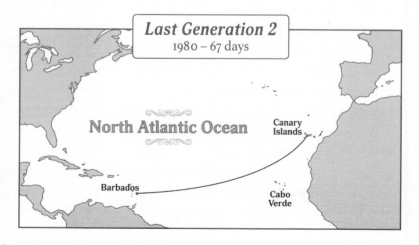

members who said women would not be able to cope with the demands of difficult and dangerous ocean crossings. I disagreed. I also felt they might be more congenial company than some of my previous male crew mates. Eventually, I decided the time had come to put my claims to the test and show that women were just as capable and courageous as men. So, I set out to find an adventurous female travel companion. Not easy in conservative Belgium. It took a while, but eventually, I found three potential candidates, hopeful that one would join my crew for *Seaview.*

They all wanted to start with the fun part, the diving lessons. Weighed down with our new diving equipment, we trekked down to the Oosterschelder River, which flowed into the North Sea. An almost deserted beach with shallow water seemed the ideal place for our first lessons. To my surprise, the women stripped off their clothes and stood disconcertingly close to me during my theoretical explanation. Helping them squeeze into their diving suits didn't help my discomfort. After teaching for two hours, it was once again time for the dressing and undressing ceremony, providing unexpected entertainment for a nearby fisherman who became so engrossed he slipped off his perch into the water.

Unfortunately, while the women were happy to join me for a voyage, they refused to do so in primitive conditions. They insisted on hotels and restaurants. Plus, their mothers were understandably sceptical about them travelling with a strange man on an unorthodox ship to a far-flung destination. There was no way this was going to work. My next step was to place an advert in a Dutch newspaper's "Travelling Companions" section, announcing that I was looking for a partner for a one-of-a-kind expedition. My message was clear: 'Let's travel each and every highway. You only live once.' I hoped that the Dutch, with their rich maritime tradition, would be more receptive to such an adventure. All I could do now was wait.

Within a week, I received 60 enthusiastic responses. I shortlisted ten and let them know that I would be interested in meeting them. Much to my astonishment, the women took the initiative and started turning up uninvited at my solitary farmhouse. Gerda turned up first. She informed me straight away that she was interested in my adventure and in getting to know me better, so she had taken a week off work to stay with me. When I pointed out that this was unexpected and I only had one bed, she coolly replied that this was the best way for us to get to know each other. I was taken aback but obliging!

After three weeks of "getting to know" various women, I was none the wiser. Despite their undeniable enthusiasm, I wasn't sure any of them would make a good crew member – and that was what it was about. My last hope was the woman who had sent the shortest letter, just two sentences scribbled on a page ripped from a notebook: 'Hello, World Traveller, if I find you as exciting as your plans and you like me too, let's go. Come and have dinner with me.'

And so, my search led me to Kee Arens from Amsterdam. Things seemed promising from the start. I had to venture out to meet her, rather than have her turn up on my doorstep uninvited. She led a busy life, and it took several weeks to arrange a meeting. When we finally got together on a frosty evening in Amsterdam, I found exactly what I was looking for: an enthusiastic, adventurous travel companion. It didn't hurt that she was also beautiful.

Kee: The "Travelling Companions" section of the paper was always my favourite page. I had replied to several ads

*like, "Travelling companion sought for an odyssey through
South America" or "Who wants to come on a world trip?"
But the meetings I had with the people involved were
always disappointing. This time, an ad for a companion to
join a unique expedition caught my attention. I replied and
thought nothing more about it until I received a phone call.*

*The caller introduced himself as Fons, a world traveller
who had crossed the ocean on a raft and was now looking
for a female crew member for his next adventure: a
journey across the Caribbean in a self-made submarine-
type vessel. Intrigued, I decided to satisfy my curiosity and
agreed to meet him. Our first encounter was on a freezing
January night. We slipped and skidded over the icy streets.
It felt like we had known each other for years, and I knew
I wanted to be with him. The next day, I handed in my
resignation to KLM Airlines, and after working my notice,
I moved to Belgium with just one suitcase to live with Fons.
I was 33 and Fons 40 years old.*

Kee and I spent many evenings discussing our impending
adventure. She asked smart questions and showed enthusiasm
for every detail, undeterred by the potential dangers and
hardships. Every conversation strengthened my conviction she
was the perfect choice of partner.

Meanwhile, as I prepared *Seaview* for travel, I gave yet another
lecture that ended in a discussion about whether a woman
would be able to cope with the primitive conditions on my ocean
rafts. I chatted to Kee about it as we sat in the sunshine next to
the BASF factory in Antwerp, where I was building *Seaview*.

'*Seaview* won't be ready for a while. What do you think about
giving the raft a go together?' I asked.

She replied without hesitation. 'Sure, why not?'

*

We had several lively discussions about renaming *Last Generation* for her second voyage. Kee wanted to call her *Fons*, saying that I'd spent so much time working on the raft she was just an extension of me. I was having none of it. *I* was Fons, not the raft!

So, that was how we found ourselves, a few weeks later, aboard *Last Generation (Definitely Not Fons)*, which had been graciously granted a free passage back from Trinidad to Antwerp ready for her new voyage. The raft pounded and swerved, refusing to cooperate as she was towed by tugboat. Water swirled wildly across the pipes. The towing was difficult and slow, and the frustrated tugboat captain shouted that a 500-tonne ship provided much less resistance than our strange raft. The tug towed us to Rotterdam, from where *Last Generation* would be carried to Las Palmas de Gran Canaria. Once again, we had managed to fix a free crossing for the raft. This time it was on a Danish cargo ship

Fons and Kee on Last Generation, *tied up in the harbour*

named the *Stjerneborg*. This time, with much still to arrange, I decided that we would fly to meet *Last Generation*.

A couple of weeks later, we were standing in a different world on the island of Gran Canaria. A storm delayed *Stjerneborg* and when it docked a week after we arrived, we were impatient for the launch of *Last Generation*. The crew lowered her into the water and we set to work repairing damage incurred in her stormy passage and preparing for our departure. Since the raft was to be our home, Kee made the canvas cabin as cosy as possible. It was always open on one side, and Kee added a beautiful, threadbare Persian rug that perfectly fitted the floor, a present from a friend, Frederico. On the port side were our sleeping quarters, a couple of thin sleeping bags zipped together on which we laid our thick sleeping bags. We placed the suitcase holding the transmitter and marine telephone in the opposite corner towards the stern, under the canvas window. We used three boxes as storage and kitchen cabinets on the right of the entrance. In front of this was the Primus stove. A backpack we had hung high up on one side served as our bookshelf and medicine cabinet. We had all sorts of army rations stored in the pipes, including a considerable quantity of biscuits as bread substitutes.

Christmas and New Year came and went, and in mid-January, we set sail. Everyone on the quayside cheered, all the boats in the harbour honked their horns, and fireworks and firecrackers went off. As we left the harbour, people were standing on the rocks waving goodbye. It was a beautiful send-off.

After such a cheery start, the voyage turned difficult quickly. The weather was sad and rainy. Wild waves came at us from the side, and the coast on our starboard appeared threatening. We hoisted our square-rigged sail. It was dark and cold. We had to shine a torch at the compass to see if we were on the right southerly course keeping clear of the coast and several exposed rocks. The strong northern wind stood us in good stead, but steering was painful. It took all our strength to haul the rudder from one side to the other, and Kee was struggling with seasickness. The wind pushed us past the coast and the pointy rocks.

By darkness, we had Gran Canaria behind us. We were safe. The wind calmed, and we could keep the rudder pretty much in one direction. We agreed that we would take one hour turns at the helm, but later in the night that became one and a half and then two hours. The tablets for seasickness worked well for me but did not affect Kee at all. Nevertheless, she was resolute and told me she had no fear. She had surrendered herself to the sea, and fully intended to fend for herself whatever happened.

Later that night, I turned on the light in our mast. Electricity came from a small generator and we had to conserve petrol,

Last Generation *underway*

so we only turned on the light when ships were nearby. A searchlight flashed across us, and a large ship came alongside. Then we were hit by another flash of light, which was a shock. I hadn't seen anything coming from behind the sail. Fortunately, the freighter ploughed right past us, but it was a harsh reminder that we were still in the shipping routes running next to Africa.

A few days later, another ship appeared from out of nowhere. It was a chance to try out our marine telephone, the VHF. They had trouble understanding us, but we could hear them clearly. I used our gas burner to solder a loose wire, fixing the VHF cable. We saw another ship, from the Congo, and when we made contact, they could hear us perfectly. Success! We asked for the position so we could check our calculations. The north latitude was correct at 27° 04'. But the west longitude differed one degree, which was about 60 nautical miles from what we had worked out. I used several methods to calculate it again but got the same result: 16° 37' W. The ship from the Congo had to be wrong. They were in for a surprise if they ended up in a different country from what they expected.

We struggled with the wrong winds and drifted sternwards and sidewards. Where was the north-east trade wind that was supposed to blow here? A solid eastern wind would be welcome. The west wind would not be a problem for a sailboat, but we could only keep our square-rigged sail in one position for the wind. That's how rafts work, after all. They can only sail with the wind behind.

When evening fell, we saw ships everywhere, suggesting we were still in the shipping lanes. Having to watch out all the time made us uneasy. Also, we were using too much of our kerosene by leaving the oil lamps on throughout the night. We had already used one litre and had only brought ten litres in total.

The ocean water was clear but incredibly salty. *Last Generation* had been washed clean of the dirty, oily harbour water from Las Palmas. At night, the sea was as smooth as glass, and we saw the stars sparkle in it. It was surreal and beautiful. A strong southerly wind blew up and took hold. This was bad news. Everything sloshed, pounded and howled on the raft, made worse by the currents pushing us back to the north.

The wind lost its strength, but the sea remained wild. It always took a few hours to calm down. Then, from out of nowhere, an easterly wind arrived. We hoisted the sail immediately and took turns standing at the helm. Navigation showed us that we had been lying still for 24 hours. At least we had not drifted backwards.

By day seven, our position was too far west. We had experienced all possible winds except the one we wanted: the northeasterly trade wind. That night we crossed the busy shipping route, and from now on we would see few or no ships.

Kee: When dawn appeared after a restless night, I washed thoroughly. Fons's idea of cleaning himself was to jump in and out of the sea. He quoted the French sailor Bernard Moitessier: 'My last soaping up was months ago, yet I do not have a single pimple on my body,' and told me about David Lewis, the New Zealander who sailed the first solo trip to Antarctica and only took off his trousers when they were threadbare. Both remained very healthy. You do not get very dirty at sea since there is no dust or smoke.

All at once, the waves came from starboard, and the wind slowly turned north-east. The miracle had happened! Time to hoist the sail.

We needed to pull up more provisions from the pipes, so Fons loosened the lids' bolts for me to crawl in and pass up the supplies. We had to throw away our stock of bread from Las Palmas, which should have lasted us a week. All that remained were soldiers' rusks. Our jerrycan was empty, and we pumped the first water from the pipe tank. It was grey-brown. We had brought coffee filters to sieve the water if needed. They turned black after a couple of splashes, but as the water passed through them it became clear, and the taste was not that terrible. In comparison, the 40 litres of mineral water in plastic bottles, which we had bought to alternate with, tasted horribly of plastic.

We made significant progress that day: 70 miles south and 30 miles west. We took a day off and lay naked in the sun, diving into the ocean from the raft with a line tied around us. It was a breathtaking experience because of the depth, the openness and the fish we encountered.

We were unlucky again with the wind. The southern breeze turned into a raging storm with foaming tops on the waves. We were in a wilderness of sounds. A high wave came from behind and dived under the raft, only to come out tall and churning at the bow seconds later. The ocean washed across the deck, rushing into our cabin and taking everything along its path. We tied the sail and yard tightly to the deck and then secured a long lifeline around ourselves. We kept our survival suits on because they were warm, and we felt safe in them. It started to rain infernally, and the cabin's sail billowed inwards with great force. It was pitch black, and we stood on the deck, anticipating possible dangers. In the middle of the night, we hung to the mast together, experiencing the furious weather. It was a relief when the day broke.

We had drifted 18 miles northwards again. The wind turned in the afternoon, making the waves hit us beam on, which was uncomfortable and dangerous. According to the pilot's guide, the wind should be almost entirely northeasterly here. It did not make any sense. The night came, bringing raging showers from the south-west, south-east and north-west. The swell was enormous. We had no way whatsoever of intervening in our situation. At least Kee was a supportive companion. It made the hard times easier. We fought over silly things but soon made up, which was just as well. I knew from experience how difficult it was not to get along in these circumstances.

Eventually, the wind calmed, and the sun shone. The seawater was a different colour, pale turquoise, with dirty objects floating around. Were we already that close to the African coast? We had just stripped off and stretched out to sunbathe, lying on the planks, when a Cabo Verdean fishing boat came around the corner of the raft at full speed. It was too late, but we threw some clothes on. There must have been 20 laughing, shouting men at the railing, and they all raised their hands and waved. Their boat was a hunk of rust, but we could still read the name: *Mieuwsie*. They disappeared towards the south.

We could keep the rudder in place using the lines, and I updated the great sea chart on which I had drawn our most likely route. I planned it on the same map as my previous crossing on *Last Generation*, so we could make comparisons. That voyage had reached approximately the same position as we had now on the 16th day, but then we had already covered 540 miles from Morocco; on this voyage, we had only done the 216 miles from Gran Canaria.

*

Day 13. Our journey became an odyssey, an ordeal for body and spirit. Raging and whistling, the roaring south wind battered our primitive raft. The vessel lost any will of her own. The fore and backstays took turns being as taut as a guitar string. Like two frightened cats, Kee and I hunkered down in the small canvas cabin that produced a whining, clanking serenade with every wind blast.

During those days, we served as playthings for nature. We hardly made any progress, and there was even a chance that the unfavourable storm winds would throw us from the trade wind route and into even worse North Atlantic weather.

The pilot charts covering the first three months of the year informed us that the direction of the currents and winds should be helpful at this time. Instead, we were hit with a roaring storm wind that stubbornly kept coming from the wrong direction. When dark and threatening cloud masses gathered on the horizon, we hardly had enough time to pull on our bright red survival suits and tie ourselves to the mast. The shrieking wind whipped the rain showers over our soaked bodies. Outside on the deck, masses of water gurgled between the planks, but it was at least better than in the cabin, where the banging canvas produced an excessive noise. The sea anchor line creaked as it tautened while the wind drove the raft north against the currents.

The next day, everything felt different: the weather, the atmosphere, as if we had broken through a weather barrier. Kee scrubbed herself with the shoe brush while I threw buckets of water over her. For the third day running, we kept a southwesterly course. February had come, and by the end of the month we would have passed our halfway point. It was sunny and there was a strong north-east wind behind us. What more could we want but a following wind? We were now at 22° 22' N. If we continued like this, we would be parallel to Cabo Verde.

It was already light at 6am, so sunrise was around 6.30am. We had to turn our watches back ten minutes. The more we went west, the earlier it was.

*

Day 23. According to the maps, a Beaufort force 4 wind was supposed to keep our sails billowing at this time, but we kept having winds of force 6 to 7. The raft bumped and rolled from left to right, pounding and struggling, and the beams made it sound like a fast train. We were now speeding along at 2.5 knots. In seven days, we had covered almost twice the distance we had done during the first 14. We concluded that we were going too far in the direction of Cabo Verde. We tightened the sheets and lowered the spare sail, which had been pushing us too far south. It was also time for some cleaning: the layer of barnacles grew thicker on the side of the raft, just as they had on my first voyage, and the whole rudder blade was covered in seaweed, as were the planks at the front between the pipes.

Kee: By day 26 I was whimpering with tiredness and seasickness. Fons was also exhausted. His left eye was swollen, and all his limbs were aching, so he couldn't sleep. That whole day we lay in bed sick, side by side, only getting out when it was necessary. The exhaustion was also mental; body and spirit are one, after all. Fons said having a man-woman crew was ideal, but I'd add that a good relationship is necessary.

After a month at sea, we saw large schools of flying fish and beautiful silver-white fish on the run from the dorados. If dorados are blue, they are not hungry and do not eat; if they turn green, they are hungry and start hunting. I was enjoying Fons's book about his first voyage on the raft. I'd read it a year ago, but now I was in the middle of this adventure, it really spoke to me.

Fons threw out the fishing line because he felt like fried fish. It quickly became taut: a large, beautiful dorado was squirming at the end. I found this cruel and burst into tears. Fons asked if I'd gone mad and wanted me to help, but I refused. The fish struggled and dived back into the water. I was still crying in the cabin, so Fons said, 'We won't be fishing anymore.' I thought that was a silly remark. I was willing to try. I just had to get used to it.

Three days later, we were woken by a squirming movement around our feet: a flying fish. Fons said, 'That is going into the pan.'

While navigating, we saw that we had covered this passage from Cabo Verde three days faster than I had done last time. We celebrated with powdered lemonade, so we hardly noticed the unpleasant taste of the water. Kee was intrigued by the barnacles on the raft's side and we found them to be strange parasites. When the water splashed over them, they stuck their little tongues out to pull in their food, the plankton in the sea.

In the mornings, we saw a lot of flying fish: breakfast time for the dorados. I made something that looked like a flying fish from a frayed rope and tied it onto a hook. We caught a dorado in no time and Kee was prepared this time. She threw herself onto the fish, even though it was at least one and a half metres long and incredibly strong.

That night, the raft swayed as never before. The waves came from the side, and because the wind had subsided, the sea's rolling was more severe, making the raft rear up terribly. We had to hold on to anything we could as we were thrown from one end of the bed to the other in the cabin. Since we had no railing, we had to watch out, or we would get thrown overboard. At night that would almost certainly have fatal consequences.

Kee's Triumph

Last Generation, Voyage 2

Day 40 was an important day: we had covered half the distance we planned for our crossing. We were still 1,350 nautical miles from Trinidad, though, and the tiller had started to tear away from the rudder. I had half expected this to happen and had a solution prepared. Before we set off, I'd drilled a hole in the rudder so I could attach a line to it. After an hour's struggle in the water with a line tied around me, wearing my diving goggles, I attached the rudder blade to both sides of the raft using two lines. The constantly jumping raft gave me a couple of bumps to the head as souvenirs of my endeavours. The tiller broke off completely at dusk, but the ropes had already taken over its function on the rudder blade. Now we were using the sail to steer, squaring the sail and the beams.

> *Kee: That week, we had two unusual encounters. The first came one day when I was on deck, wearing only my straw boater, and I felt large spatters of water on my back. 'Funny, Fons,' I said. But, seconds later, I spotted an enormous shark in the water next to me, beating its tail back and forth. 'A shark!' I shouted excitedly. It must have been four metres long and, except for a white stomach, was grey all over.*

It scraped its belly against the raft and swam around us several times. The dorados just stayed where they were, giving it sideways glances to watch its moves. We got a jolt every time it scraped its stomach against our pipes. It was sad to see it disappear abruptly into the depths again.

Our second encounter was with the 240-metre crude oil carrier Burmah Peridot. *We'd spotted a ship in the distance on day 44 and tried desperately to get their attention. We were keen to hand over the letters we'd written and, more importantly, to ask for some drinking water. After a number of attempts, they finally saw us and agreed to help. Excitement filled the air as the massive tanker adjusted course and approached us. We quickly tied a rope to our mast and exchanged greetings with the Chinese crew members. Fons worked hard to ensure our safety, placing fenders between the raft and the ship. We had a moment of panic when the rope connecting us snapped, but the crew swiftly threw us new lines. They provided us with much-needed drinking water and even dropped empty containers for us to fill. On top of that, they gave us two bottles of whisky to open when we arrived, two cans of beer, two tins of corned beef, a big bag of tortilla chips, five white cabbages, four grapefruits, fourteen oranges and many more vegetables and fruit. What a fantastic treat! We bid farewell to the crew, hugely grateful for their generosity and support. I told Fons I would happily spend all my life at sea to have such an experience once in a while.*

All night, the sea was calm, and we drifted over the vast, moonlit ocean covered with sparkling stars. We sat cross-legged, facing each other in the moonlight and talking about our lives. This raft voyage had already proved that we were well-suited to living together. Fons said that every couple who wanted to live together should start drifting around on a raft for a month.

To mark our crossing of the 40th latitude, we threw a message into the sea in a bottle. We put in a photo and promised the finder $20 if they sent us a letter. Little did we know that this simple act was going to change our lives later, inspiring us to design our own bottle-shaped boat!

Our spirits were high. I felt accustomed to the sea. Every day, I was busy. I was never bored or upset. Fons took the transparent plastic box where we had kept the compass and made it into a diorama for looking underwater. By holding a camera in the box, he could take underwater photos. Together we lay next to the opening in the deck and looked at the fish. That was the advantage of having no wind. But it was scorching. There was hardly any shade since the sun was so high, so with lifelines and goggles, we jumped into the ocean. The fish just came to us, undaunted. It was gorgeous under the raft covered with green weed, and I could see 30 metres into the depths in the clear water.

During navigation, we discovered we had covered the same distance in two days that we had previously done in one: 31 nautical miles. The sea was as smooth as glass. But then the raft began to sway intensely, and small wild waves from the south came sloshing against our port side. It felt as though a fight was taking place underwater. Most likely, it was a case of different currents meeting up on that spot. Up in the mast, I tossed to and fro and had to hold on tight to avoid falling out. The sail hung like a towel against the stays. When we looked under the raft, there was a hive of activity. There must have been 30 dorados, a whole group of triggerfish and a pilot fish.

*

1 March. Day 49. There was a good chance we would see land this month: Barbados was our hope. It was two degrees less to the west than Trinidad, and one of the ham radio enthusiasts we had been talking to said he had friends there who might come and meet us with their boat to tow us in. The currents around these islands were strong, and impossible to steer accurately with the raft. We could arrive in three weeks if we were lucky with the wind.

> *Kee: We had brought a Spanish course on cassette tapes because Fons was determined to learn the language. However, he never made it past the first five sentences, of which he knew one best and therefore said it regularly: 'Yo soy un hombre.' (I am a man). I wasn't sure that would take him far. It had rather limited opportunities for use.*

That night, the moon rose complete and huge, leaving a golden sea behind the raft. Kee was standing on the back deck playing her recorder while I experimented with filming and photography. In the middle of the night, a sudden clattering shower came, together with strong blasts of wind. We worried about how the sail would hold up during those gale force 8 blasts, but we couldn't take it down. The tremendous pulling power made the sheets shake. All we could do was wait to see what happened, hoping it would end well. After half an hour, Lady Luck stood by us, the wind subdued, and the air cleared.

The weather remained volatile and we noticed a dark, menacing cloud approaching from a distance. This was almost always a forewarning of one of the storms that regularly occur south of the 20th northern latitude, often termed tornadoes. When ominous cumulonimbus clouds appeared in the east and the wind fell silent, it was time to watch out. As the cloud masses came closer, they would grow denser and darker, bringing either thunder and lightning or massive wind blasts. We had to lower the sail quickly and pull it between the sheets to tie it down.

This time, we were ready just in time to face the assault. It was quite an experience, so much rain in the middle of the day. Kee met it on deck, naked, wanting to feel the full force of nature and bathe in the rainwater. I stood next to her, happier in a raincoat as the rain was freezing. After half an hour, the storm had passed and we hoisted the sail again. The sun came back just in time for our navigation, and there were only sheep-like clouds in the sky.

We relaxed in the cabin and made the big mistake of not paying attention to our surroundings during the night. After a while, I went outside to check on the state of the world and yelled for Kee as I saw a red and green light with two white ones in between – collision course! I connected the VHF to warn the ship that we were right in front of them. Kee ran to the deck with the generator and saw the green starboard light very close to us, indicating that the ship would narrowly miss us. We heard the VHF calling us. They asked who we were and told us they had spotted us at the last moment and abruptly changed course. We were incredibly lucky, and I thanked them sincerely for their alertness. Their enormous bow wave threw the raft in all directions as they passed.

We started to keep a proper watch again. Being in the middle of the ocean without seeing a ship for so long had reduced our alertness. Now we had to look every half hour to see if the coast was clear and if we were still following the right course, to check how the sail and stays were holding up, and to make sure there was no storm coming our way.

*

Day 52. When we saw massive grey cloud decks heading towards us, we grabbed our coats, lowered our sail and surrendered to the rainstorm and hurricane-like wind. Later, as we were checking the stays, I tripped and tumbled overboard. I managed to grab the end of the beam that was sticking out over the edge and clamped myself onto the wood with my legs dragging in the water. I pulled myself up and when I was safely back on deck, Kee held on to me tightly and wouldn't let go. She didn't look particularly reassured when I told her, 'I was holding on, though.'

One week later, we were cheered by the realisation that Barbados was now the closest country. It had been French Guyana until then. The weather was terrific, with waves topped with friendly white foam, and there was an intense sparkling glow over the deep blue water. The dorados jumped around us, and Kee and I both took a moment to acknowledge that, even though we were becoming used to it, this was a very special way of life.

Soon we came into the solid southern current that runs alongside the Brazilian coast towards the Caribbean. We still could not say for sure where we would end up, although we had high hopes of being in Barbados within six days. I spoke on the VHF to Pat in Barbados, who asked for the colour of the raft and the sail so those who would come looking for us could identify us.

The next few days seemed unbearably long because we were ready to see land but still couldn't. As a distraction, I decided to fix the rudder, so I attached the tiller using threaded rods that I had bent into the shape of a clamp. Now we could hold the tiller and the piece on top of the rudder. It was a solid construction.

Three porpoises appeared. They were new to us, and it was beautiful to see them dive with long, undulating movements. We could just about see their backs above the water, nothing more. Our dorados were nowhere to be seen, but they came back as soon as the porpoises had disappeared. We had covered 80 miles, the most significant distance our raft had ever done in one day. Then again, we'd had stormy winds day and night. We were just 180 miles to Barbados, but we still weren't sure we would arrive on the island. The most powerful currents in that area could drive us into the Caribbean Sea. The radio hams would be on standby from the day after tomorrow, Monday.

Radio Barbados cheered us up. They always started the day with 'Good morning, folks, another day in paradise.' Despite this, Kee and I had one of our rare quarrels. As the sun went down behind the sail, Kee fumbled with the stays and took so long that I missed the opportunity to take a reading, which was infuriating so close to our arrival. Then Kee snapped at me for snapping at her. A little later, I was still ready for battle, but when she barked, 'Hurry up, man, we're on the wrong course,' I had to laugh. It was impossible to stay angry with Kee. She was my best mate and best crew member, even when she was telling me off.

> *Kee: I felt emotional because our voyage had almost reached its end, I had settled into our life at sea, just the two of us. Maybe we would see things differently after this experience and become more grateful for the little things in life. It was good to discover that Fons and I had grown closer despite everything. We were sitting on the fore deck in the wind, letting the foaming water wash over us while we enjoyed the last rays of the sun. What could be more*

beautiful? The only thing that could make it more perfect would be the sight of land in the distance.

In the middle of the night, around 2am, Fons yelled that we had to lower the sail fast. We could see the outline of a black mass against the dark grey sky: another terrible squall. It was a struggle in the darkness. We were almost blown over and flooded. When our distress was finally over, and Fons hoisted the sail, we both fell into a deep sleep.

I woke up in shock more than two hours later. We had not looked outside for all that time. It could have been the end of us.

The next day, we were shocked to see our position; the currents had dragged the raft 34 miles south. This was a disaster, and we were now 13 miles under Barbados. We had wasted our luck with the easterly wind and were promptly given a northeasterly. There was no way we could get back up with that. I was worried. Our position had been so good, and these last two days, we were supposed to have descended slowly. According to the chart, we should have had a strong upward current here. But the opposite appeared to be the case, and we were in a southerly current taking us towards Grenada. That was another three days of sailing and not where we wanted to go.

We had good contact with Pat on the VHF, and he said he would come to meet us with boats. The coastguard would pick us up no more than 30 miles off the coast. Radio Barbados was ready and waiting on channel 16. Anglers along the coast were looking out for us.

The dark clouds and the wind whipping us further south worsened matters. We felt foolish for keeping such a low course, although it later turned out to have been our salvation since we would otherwise have sailed on to the coral reefs. Trying our hardest, we squared sails and steered using the rudder, but the sail could not handle a course of more than 290° before blowing shut. Reefing the spare sail helped a little, but then the sail slammed shut again. I had to hold back the plank while Kee quickly tightened the braces. It was impossible. The wind knocked everything out of our hands, and I couldn't pull hard enough. We tried, and we kept on trying, using all our strength, until finally it worked. While Kee used the ropes to reinforce the beam, I took a measurement of the polar star. The calculations showed that we had risen a little. At a quarter past five that morning, I checked again and reached the same result as the evening before: 12° 55' N.

Pat said we should try to reach Radio Barbados using the VHF.

'Radio Barbados, Radio Barbados, this is the raft on the Atlantic Ocean. Do you copy us? Over.'

We waited, static filling the air, until it morphed into a friendly voice: '*Last Generation,* this is Radio Barbados. I copy you. The coastguard will leave at eight o'clock.' The friendly voice on the radio added that a small aircraft would soon be in the air, looking for us.

We heard a growing roar. The small aeroplane had spotted us. It flew low above us a couple of times and then kept circling. We waved anything we could find in the air and cast out the sea anchor, hoping they were relaying our position to the coastguard. As the northeasterly wind strengthened, pushing us further away, we watched the island's lights shift to the right and then fade. We had passed it. Every few minutes, I cast a worried glance towards the disappearing lights of Barbados.

The next day, Radio Barbados informed us that a cabin cruiser, the *Countrygirl,* was heading our way. I kept a constant watch with the binoculars while Kee handled the radio. A few minutes later, they asked if we could spot the cruiser since they thought they might have seen our mast. We thought that was unlikely – nobody ever saw us because we were so small. Yet suddenly there it was, the cruiser looming into view, coming straight at us, with a broad-shouldered red-blond man at the helm and another four men on board.

We laughed, waved and shouted, 'Hello, hello, how are you? We are so glad to see you.'

We were saved!

The men on the cruiser threw a thick towing line toward us. We had a good speed heading towards Bridgetown. Water fizzed over the pipes, and behind us the wake swirled. The whole island had heard about our arrival, and many people came towards us in their boats.

Slowly, the dull grey of the land bloomed green, and we began to distinguish hills, trees and buildings. After seven hours

Countrygirl *tows* Last Generation *towards Bridgetown*

of towing, it was almost 5pm. Softly we docked and moored the raft on the quay. The experience was unreal. A lady stretched her hand out to Kee and said, 'Welcome to Barbados.' And we set foot on land for the first time in 67 days.

For the second time, *Last Generation* had carried my crew and me safely across the Atlantic. It was Kee's first crossing, but she had proved herself to be not just a reliable crew member, but a stalwart companion. Her fortitude and resilience had been my beacon of hope in the expansive and often relentless ocean. Kee had become the first woman on record to cross the Atlantic Ocean on a raft.

Steam Boiler at Sea

Seaview

January 1981, *Seaview* set sail from Cabo Verde carrying me, Kee and three extra crew. After three weeks we were making good albeit ponderous progress on our westerly journey. The 15-metre vessel was a bizarre and ungainly T-shaped construction. It consisted of a reclaimed steam boiler with an underwater observation chamber built on to the underside, created from a propane gas tank that was originally six metres long, or rather, once attached, six metres deep. The resulting contraption completely ignored traditional ship-building conventions but was a triumph of ingenuity. She shocked sceptics as she glided slowly but effortlessly on the trade winds across tropical waters 600 nautical miles north of the Equator. It had been a monumental task to turn her into a reliable, functional, and seaworthy vessel, but despite the cloudy predictions from many interested parties, I had stubbornly continued construction. Much to the amazement of all, the waterline, which I had applied based on my careful calculations, touched the water precisely.

I thought of all this now, as I sat below in the observation chamber, immersed in an underwater world, studying the luminescent plankton and hostile waters through round, 2.5-centimetre thick armoured glass windows. Our watertight, 400-watt searchlights had once been the landing lights of a DC3-aircraft, but now clawed greedily into the dark mass of water, casting a secretive, magical light on the ocean's mystery, creating a panorama of the breathtaking beauty and diversity of life it contained. In tight formation, blue dorados slid close to the glass, fluttering between the small, brown triggerfish whose tiny, spout-like mouths bit at the barnacles that grew around the windows, while strange eel-like shapes slipped in and out of view. Other ocean inhabitants rose from the eternal darkness to feed themselves from the surface waters of the North Equatorial Current. At the first sign of the dangerous daylight, they would descend back into their world where crushing water pressure reigned.

I found myself drawing comparisons between my own journey and Jules Verne's *Twenty Thousand Leagues Under the*

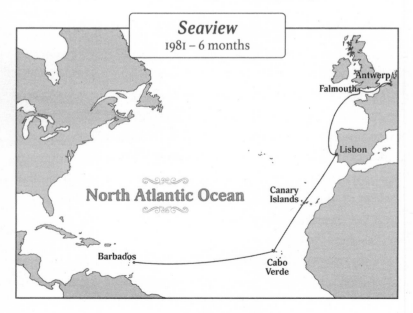

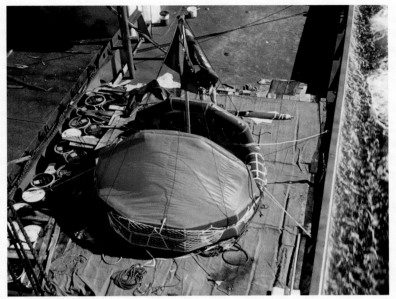

Atlantis | *Loaded onboard Mobeko underway to the Canary Islands.*

Atlantis | *Being lowered into the Atlantic. 'None of the crew gave us any chance of surviving'.*

Atlantis | *Liferaft after launch steered by Fons.*

Last Generation Voyage I | *Hassan Fishing.*

Last Generation Voyage 1 | *Fons flanked by crewmates Hassan and Raoul.*

Last Generation Voyage 2 | *Kee writing about the voyage.*

Last Generation Voyage 2 | *Kee in the raft's canvas cabin preparing a simple meal.*

Last Generation Voyage 2 | *Kee and Fons in Barbados.*

Seaview | *Fons on radio call to nearby shipping.*

Seaview | *Perched in hatch Fons studying chart.*

Seaview | *Underway with sails unfurled.*

Seaview | *Diving to inspect propeller and rudder.*

Seaview | *Bjorn Tore Holtet shooting the sun. Frank Robertson in cockpit.*

Seaview | *Cunard liner QEII passes close by to give passengers a view.*

Seaview | *Under twin sails with a following wind.*

Seaview | *Anchored in Barbados and a local tourist attraction.*

Sea, which I had devoured in my youth. Verne described how the *Nautilus*'s crew gazed at the ocean life through three-metre windows, at great depths, and at a distance of up to a kilometre around the submarine. But from behind the round windows of my *Seaview*, I knew that to be impossible. The immense water pressure would have blasted through those large windows and floodlights, however powerful, do not penetrate far into the sea. Our experience seemed far more tangible, but like the characters in the fictional *Nautilus*, we too watched the ocean life through large glass walls.

Long before, and during the construction of *Seaview*, I was preoccupied with planning and designing a small submarine capable of reaching a depth of 100 metres. My plan was to explore the bottom of the North Sea and find remains of Second World War fighters like Hawker Hurricanes, Supermarine Spitfires (especially those with their mighty Merlin Engines), American Thunderbolts and bombers like Lancasters, and the B17 Flying Fortress. This quest was driven by my interest in flying machines, which I built myself. Sadly although I never abandoned the idea, I had no time to complete the construction of a true submarine.

On my raft, *Last Generation,* my fascination with marine life had come alive and the idea of being able to watch it close up became an obsession. Once again, I chose the most challenging route. My first concept involved a floating tower with two-thirds of its height submerged, providing below-the-waterline decks for observations. I named this curious vertical vessel *SeaLab* and came up with two design versions. When *SeaLab* turned out to be impractical, I turned my attention to developing an unconventional vessel around an old steam boiler. I again discarded the security of existing designs, and stubbornly pursued a dream project that was deemed unviable by other people, which made it difficult to find sponsors.

I remained determined to design and build a vessel that could slowly almost drift across the Atlantic, providing views of marine life just below the surface. And so *Seaview* was born. Constructing her was to prove a monumental undertaking that was far more difficult than building a small sub.

The massive 30-year-old steam boiler, an unwieldy colossus from a Leeds' factory hall, was laboriously cut into three manageable chunks using a heavy blow torch. It had a wall thickness of just over two centimetres, held together with double rows of heavy bolts. I divided it into cabins, an engine room, a storage area and communal spaces. Then, using the donated, nearly new propane tank made of nine-millimetre-thick steel, I started work constructing and assembling the most exciting section, the underwater observatory.

If you want to displace a tank vertically through the water and propel it for a distance of over 5,000 nautical miles, it has to be streamlined. My solution involved attaching two-centimetre thick steel plates behind the tank so this underwater section would form the shape of a teardrop and be perfectly streamlined. The next job was the glass panes. A specialised glazier in Antwerp provided three armoured windows that would offer us an unprecedented view of the ocean's depths.

The Antwerp harbour authorities offered the use of a wharf by the water. A crane placed the unwieldy boiler sections and the underwater tank in their correct sequence, forming the giant T-shaped construction. Two welding specialists equipped with sophisticated machinery sealed the large joints. We used measuring equipment with ultrasonic vibrations to check all

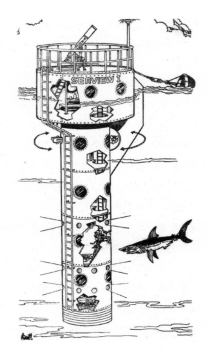

*Two design versions of SeaLab.
The vertical SeaLab was
conceived as a floating laboratory
with underwater viewing
capabilities. However, SeaLab
faced its own set of problems
during testing. This prompted
further evolution in my designs
into the more practical vessel that
I named Seaview.*

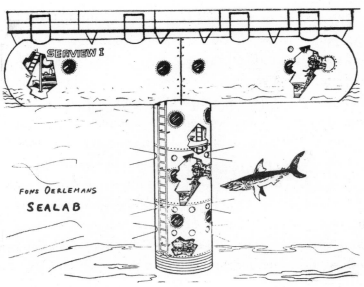

joints carefully. Next, I installed the three underwater windows, placing a thick seal between the glass and the frames and tightening the flanges. Unfortunately, a crack appeared in one layer of the front glass, which would have posed a formidable challenge if we'd had to replace it underwater.

Finally, more than two years after construction began, *Seaview* was ready to be tested on water. A crowd of onlookers watched as an enormous 70-tonne crane carefully lifted the giant orange vessel above the dock water before letting her slowly descend. Though she floated beautifully, we needed at least another five tonnes of ballast, bringing the total to seven tonnes. Fortunately, I did not know at the time that it would take three more years before *Seaview* would sail out of the Port of Antwerp. We discovered that the original observation chamber gave *Seaview* an enormous draught of five metres. Once afloat and under power there was too much resistance underwater

Seaview *before launching*

for *Seaview* to move through the water. I decided to cut off two metres from the underwater chamber, which we did with *Seaview* hanging from a crane.

Seaview would be powered by a 120 horsepower truck engine I had adapted for maritime use when the currents and wind came from the wrong direction. During the following months, the 12-metre steel mast, the pipe construction of the deck, the cabins, and the railing were constructed and installed. The initial temporary deck, made of planks, was replaced by metal grids, allowing ocean water to flow through without resistance.

Once, while running over the thin deck pipes, I slipped and smacked into a steel crosspiece and hung semi-conscious on a tiny tube above the water. Despite agonising pain, I managed to drag myself back onto the deck. I was alone – Eric had just left and wasn't expected back that day. Hours later, I made it to my car and drove to the doctor, where I was diagnosed with concussion and two broken ribs. The doctor prescribed a month of bed rest – I was not able to comply.

Seaview now had a fantastic berth in the docks at the BASF, and it was time to provide some urgent improvements. I fixed the underwater window and added a streamlined bow to reduce resistance, using massive beams and plates to construct a watertight, cone-shaped bow, which also served as a drinking water reservoir. After slogging away for months, we reached the point where *Seaview* could be lowered into the dock for the second time.

Despite her heavy bow, our strange ship lay perfectly level in the water. Gliding away from the quay with a force 4 wind, we steered the uncooperative 40-tonne steam boiler through the docks. The rigging and sails worked perfectly and despite the delays in the manoeuvres I was delighted with the possibilities. The main part of the long journey would be on the open seas, where discrepancies along our general course would not be too punishing.

*

Kee and I took on three extra crew. Paul from Amsterdam was technically savvy, worked hard and was very friendly. Don and Kees, microbiologists from Utrecht, wanted to participate in the journey to carry out specific tests for their university. After a successful trial run, our determination to depart that year intensified.

> *Kee: Sometimes, while we were waiting, we visited Agatha, Fons's ex-wife, and their children. These were cosy evenings, sitting around the table together sharing school stories and playing board games. But soon it was time to leave for our departure point in Antwerp and carry out our final checks.*
>
> *From the day of our first press conference onboard Seaview, crowds lined up on the quay and I regularly found myself acting as a guide to curious onlookers. Excitement built as we arranged supplies for the journey. A generous Kenwood representative loaned us a good receiver with a transmitter installation. Their technical service team provided instructions and joined us for a celebratory drink on board.*
>
> *A shipyard director we knew arranged the last few matters for us. We now had 2,000 litres of diesel in the tanks and the five of us had life-saving gear including survival suits and an inflatable life raft. Tension grew as departure loomed, but our tight-knit group made the intense preparations manageable.*
>
> *Fons let the wave of stress flow over him, maintaining his role as our steady helmsman. The grand send-off, to*

emotional hugs, cheering and applause was captured by a television crew. Despite challenging weather conditions and concerns about the depth of the water with Seaview's *six-metre draught, we stood together as one soaked bunch in the cabin and everyone remained cheerful as we embarked on our journey. Six days later, we arrived in sunny Falmouth and could finally take off our survival suits. The following day after a much-needed shower at the Royal Cornwall Yacht Club, we headed into town to check out the English faces, enjoy the Cornish pasties, call our families and give interviews to the BBC and ITV.*

Winter was approaching as we set sail from Falmouth in drizzle, shrouded by fog. Storms were forecast, but we couldn't keep waiting. A small fleet of ships escorted us out until *Seaview* headed into open sea – at which point waves came from all directions, creating chaos in the cabins, where everything was thrown hither and thither. Nobody could sleep because whenever we tried, we were hurled out of our bunks. Getting dressed felt like an acrobatic exercise. Using the engine, we covered 120 miles in two and a half days against the current and the winds. Suddenly the wind fell away, but it soon developed into a storm. When gale force winds raged, cooking was impossible, but at least we could stop the engine and sail with a storm jib and reefed mainsail, enjoying the relative quiet after all the mechanical noise. Of course, it meant going much slower, and when the wind turned, the engine had to be restarted to tack, so we started to roll again.

The heavy clouds made it impossible to navigate using the sextant. The winds shifted restlessly and we heard through the world receiver that there were furious storms in Ireland. Soon, the storm jib was torn to shreds. It was a struggle to get it down, and we had to be extremely careful not to be dragged off the deck, as the grey, foaming sea would easily swallow us. We were tired but could not sleep and fell out of our bunks repeatedly as the storm kept blowing. That night, an enormous wave crashed over the mainsail, ripping it. It took all our strength to lower. Don and Kees sewed the enormous piece of canvas back together on the pitching deck until, three-quarters of an hour later, our mainsail was standing tall once more. I manoeuvred *Seaview* back on course, although steering without a jib was a challenge. As the weather cleared, I was finally able to confirm our navigation using the sextant. Our progress was disheartening; we had covered only 35 miles in the struggle and were in the heart of sea area Finisterre, surrounded by storm warnings.

Finally, the day arrived when we could open the hatch of our clammy cabins and let in some air. The deck soon looked like a laundry with clothes flapping around in the breeze, but at least cooking was finally back on the agenda. We tuned into amateur radio operators every day and discovered that they were always keen to talk. One radio ham in Las Palmas, Lolina, wanted to know all about our ship to let the Canary Islands' newspapers and TV stations know we were coming, so I asked Kee to explain in Spanish. It later turned out that, in her poor Spanish, she had informed them we were sailing not in a steam boiler with sails but in a pressure cooker with a tea cosy. Still, at least word of our voyage was getting out.

*

Our trials weren't over. A ferocious westerly storm made the steering heavy and caused *Seaview* to rock heavily. But our encounters with sea life en route were incredible. Paul and Don saw a whale, its hushed breathing mingling with the sound of the sea, and looking through the portholes in our sleeping cabins, we could see under the water and up to the sky. We became more adept at living at sea, and while it was rarely comfortable, it came with a sense of freedom.

> *Kee, 10 November 1981: In our wildly swaying bed, in wet clothes, Fons took me by surprise by asking me to marry him. Of course, I said YES!*
>
> *But any opportunity to celebrate was swallowed by the storm from hell. Our good jib was shredded, and we almost shared its fate trying to lower the sail. Completely exhausted, we sought solace in sleep, but it was impossible when we kept rolling out of bed. As on the raft journey, I was plagued by seasickness, and despite our best efforts, we only covered 29 miles over two days, less progress than on either of the previous days. I felt half-dead, and my contribution to group morale was not fantastic: a weary cycle of doing my watch and trying to rest. Fons improved our sleeping arrangements by nailing a higher plank to the side of our bed, creating a sort of box that we could snugly fit into. Despite the grime of my survival suit and my unkempt hair, Fons said I had never looked sexier.*

At the helm, amid the ocean's roar and the ship's rumble, I had the sense of shooting across the ocean at a tremendous speed. Yet, looking over my shoulder at our wake, I was shocked to find it almost non-existent. If we carried on like this, it could take another 30 days to reach the Canary Islands. Columbus sailed it three times faster! Still, as the wind dropped, the sea became smooth and the air clear. We saw beautiful sunrises, shared meals together, and even dived into the breathtakingly cold ocean. There were moments of unexpected joy, such as our encounter with the enormous luxury cruise ship, *Queen Elizabeth II*. The captain explained that they had deviated from their course to see what was bobbing along in the distance. Although *Seaview's* length was only 15 metres compared with the QE2's 294 metres, none of the passengers peering down at us could have guessed that we had an observation chamber well below our own waterline. There were a lot of people at the railing as we hollered back and forth, and they shot a gun salute as a goodbye. They were also heading for Barbados, and the captain said: 'We'll see you there at Christmas, then.' As it turned out, we would not see the giant cruiser in Barbados until Easter. By that time, they had already been back and forth five times!

As night fell, we found ourselves surrounded by an array of ships, mainly fishing boats. We had unwittingly drifted easterly towards the Portuguese coast, covering a depressing 20 miles in two days. A thick mist engulfed us. We turned on our navigational lights and honked the horn at regular intervals as we swayed and rolled our way forth. The only comfort was the fact that, while there were storm warnings everywhere else, it was due to be calmer in sea area Trafalgar, where we were. Our struggles with the sails were rewarded during a torrential downpour by the appearance of the much-needed northwesterly wind. When the sun started to shine, we immediately felt better. Kee suggested we sleep with our cabin cover open to get some fresh air, unlike the others who kept their stuffy cabins closed.

I received regular weather updates from José, a radio operator from Belgium, who said it would take a while to get favourable winds and suggested we proceed using the engine. But our fuel reserves were dwindling, so I decided to divert course to Lisbon to top up. Since Portugal had never been a part of our plan, we had no maps or pilot charts of this area. On a clear, calm night, we moored by the Portuguese coast before continuing our journey up the River Tagus towards Lisbon, guided by instinct and hope, as we knew nothing about the water's depth. We berthed opposite the monument of Henry the Navigator, among brightly painted fishing boats and stares from curious locals.

Kee: None of us felt particularly happy about the unexpected stop, so Kees bought a bottle of red wine for us to drink together. After the first sip, everyone spewed it back out. The bottle said, "Vinaigre Vino Tinto"; Kees had purchased a bottle of vinegar! The laughter eased the tension. The unexpected delays we'd had due to the lousy weather meant Don and Kees had to return to their university commitments and Paul needed to head off too, leaving Fons and I with no choice but to sail the heavy, often uncontrollable vessel to the Canary Islands alone.

The boys slept on board for another couple of days to get to know Lisbon. I rowed them ashore for their nocturnal girl-chasing adventures, after which they'd return and whistle from the quay at 4am, expecting me to get out of bed to pick them up again! During the day, Don and Kees helped restock our water and gas supplies, while Paul and I went looking for oil.

While Fons and I topped up the oil in the engine room and ended up covered in black sludge, the boys were out enjoying Lisbon's nightlife.

I spent a whole afternoon at the Embassy of Cabo Verde, renewing our expired visas. When I whistled from the quay, Fons rowed quickly towards me, worried I'd been gone for so long. My overly enthusiastic leap into the boat resulted in an unexpected capsizing. But despite the mishaps, our spirits remained unbroken and with Kees, Paul and Don leaving us, we settled into Paul's bunk in the most stable and cosy cabin, ready for the journey that lay ahead.

At dawn on 5 December, we sailed out of the Tagus. While I was resting, there was a hard jolt, as *Seaview* lurched starboard and ran aground. I moved to help Kee at the helm, turning *Seaview* 180°, giving full throttle, and tearing at the rudder. The engine roared, and eventually we managed to free ourselves and were floating again. There were no buoys or signs anywhere. A pilot boat came rushing towards us and stayed behind us to ensure we steered a safe course along the northern coast. After three hours, we rounded the lighthouse and the ocean stretched out before us. Plastic bags, empty cans and oil drums, rags and other litter from the Tagus floated all around us, and birds rested on bits of rubbish in the water.

Steering the ship without the extra help took some getting used to. We were completely skewed when the waves came towards us from the side. Packets of flour stored above our bed tore open and covered the cabin in white powder. Everything fell or broke, even though it had been attached well. We just left everything where it had landed until the sea was calmer.

When calm finally arrived, we could sit on a small seat in front of the wheel and steer with our feet. But before long the tranquil days gave way to an ominous, sand-filled Sirocco storm from the Sahara, which covered the ship with a layer of sand for days. Not long after that, a pipe from the oil pressure gauge burst, spewing oil in all directions. Kee was left standing in the black sludge with a cup, trying to scoop up the oil into a can. Luckily, the others had left behind some of their clothes and sheets, which soon became rags for dabbing and polishing.

Finally, we saw the lights of Las Palmas in the distance, and after manoeuvring through the reef, rocks and currents, we navigated *Seaview*, aptly named the 'Ocean Steamer' by the media, through tightly-packed docks. We had arrived!

Window into the Deep
Seaview

Lolina, our friendly radio operator, had been waiting for us since 5am. When people talked about us as if we were crazy, she kept saying: 'No, those people know how to live.' We were photographed and interviewed with TV crews coming on board to film. All day long, we talked to people. By the time we fell into bed, we were exhausted. Out on the streets, people asked us if we were from the "Submarino". One day, returning to our ship, we found a cryptic message on the handrail: 'We would like to talk to you.'

While I was working on the streamlined bow under the ship, a sharply-dressed man called Marcel dropped by. He was a Belgian expat who had lived here for 15 years with his Spanish wife and child. Marcel was one of a group who planned to transport drinking water from Madeira to the Canary Islands and wanted me to build them a giant floating structure, composed of two large kettles with a smaller one in between. They imagined an engine at the rear and a steering cabin on top, and they had grand plans of transporting five million litres of water in each consignment. It seemed ambitious, but I agreed to consider it.

Here in Las Palmas, I seemed to have become the go-to guy for all kinds of boating people, but there were some jobs I wouldn't take. One was a paid diving job to retrieve a sunken anchor of a beautiful Danish three-master, travelling for four months with a group of teenage girls with behavioural issues. The hard work on board was supposed to be part of their therapy. Later, we heard the ship was delayed because some of the girls had escaped and hidden on the island to party.

We met a group of Norwegians from a beautiful fishing boat, *Viking Senior*. They had answered an ad seeking people for a cruise to Australia and had each paid 6,000 kroner, only for it to emerge that the owner was on the run from the Norwegian tax authorities and had gone into hiding in Australia. He wanted his boat there and had cleverly organised a paid trip to transport it.

> *Kee: Our days were filled with endless distractions, and we yearned for time to focus on ourselves. Fons and I had only known each other for 11 months. Admittedly, we'd experienced more in that period than most couples do in a decade together, but with different people always claiming us for one thing or another, we needed to take the time to let each other feel loved.*

I tried to start work on *Seaview*, but people kept turning up, and it wasn't easy to just turn them away. Marcel kept asking when I could start building the gargantuan floating water kettles, offering Kee and me a house and whatever we wanted financially. But it was all going a bit too fast, and the *Seaview* project had to remain our priority.

Then Marcel went missing, only to turn up in prison for art forgery. Shortly afterwards, I was surprised to find myself discussing the water project with Marcel's colleagues when I stepped out of the shower in the Royal Gran Canaria Yacht Club. They had followed me into the shower area to let me know the water project had to go through and that they were still very interested. I visited Marcel in jail, but with everything else that was going on, I didn't have time to think about the water project and was glad I never heard about it again. It was one less thing to worry about!

*

Frank and Björn, two of the Norwegians from the Viking ship, had taken a job selling fur coats – in that heat! They asked if they could sail with us to the Cabo Verde islands. This made sense. Björn was a handy, technical man and Frank was a good diver, so we bid Las Palmas goodbye and set sail for Cabo Verde.

Figuring out our best sail configurations, we estimated that it would take us two weeks to arrive at Cabo Verde. I spent a lot of time in the underwater observation compartment, studying the depths and experimenting with filming. At night, the plankton lit up. There was so much of it, and it looked like little white spirals and sometimes long, rolled-up strands, over half a metre in length. *Seaview*'s wake left a trail of golden, sparkling water.

One night we were hooted out of our beds three times by Björn. He had adjusted our course too much, and the sails were flapping shut. It was an almost impossible task to get them right again, so I switched on the engine to lie to the wind and tack. Despite the problems we ran into, and our struggles with howling winds, torn sails and injuries, we were progressing well, albeit with our world tilted at quite an angle.

Keen to document our adventure, Kee blew up our inflatable boat and Frank and I jumped into it to take photos of *Seaview* from a distance. We took the paddles and an outboard motor. The outboard motor kept stalling, but we found we could row as fast as *Seaview* was travelling. Afterwards, I jumped into the sea with my goggles, snorkel and flippers. People were often surprised to learn I couldn't swim, but I was fine in flippers.

As we drew closer to Cabo Verde, the sea once again became wild and *Seaview* started rolling. While I was sleeping, I hit the plank at the side of the bed so hard it broke off and I toppled out onto the floor. Nobody could get any rest.

We were now close to the Cabo Verde island of São Vicente. The towering cliffs made us anxious that we would run against them. The closer we came to the rocks, the more terrifying they looked, but we navigated well. According to the charts, a lonely, pointed rock with a lighthouse should mark the port entrance. We sailed closer to the coast until we saw the rock rise from the water. We had to make sure we were inside the bay before dark as the water was only nine metres deep at this point. Suddenly, a storm-like wind started to blow, threatening to tear the genoa from the boom. We dragged it down just in time but it was a tense moment. We were almost blown from the ship as we tried to be everywhere, all at once. But despite the rough weather and near misses, we managed to dock at Mindelo and the locals greeted us warmly. The fact that the boys had no visas was no problem. Everything was friendly and easy-going and the immigration people gave them the necessary paperwork without hassle. An official turned up with the Cabo Verdean flag, asking for 2,000 escudos for his pocket. We had no objection since the people there earned little and we didn't need to pay port fees.

The harbour became very lively as ships arrived from the other islands. I was amazed by how many languages the locals could communicate. Even in Japanese and Korean, the very countries had emptied the seas here. The local inhabitants had no work themselves because there were so few fish left to be caught in these overfished waters.

A young Belgian called Alex came to visit. His boat was moored nearby and when we went to visit him on board, we were entertained by his predicament. He'd previously been moored at the quay, but after being pursued by a group of lusty local women, he'd become so exhausted that he had dropped anchor as far as possible into the bay. But it was no use. The women swam out and threw themselves at him, once again. He blamed the lack of men on the island – one for every ten women, because they left for work. On hearing this, Björn and Frank were keen to moor our rubber dinghy there as quickly as possible.

*

On 18 February, we departed from São Vicente, watching it slowly disappear like a jagged ghost island as we set our westward course. The sea was rough between the islands. We set a course of 290° due west since there was a 20° deviation. Behind Santo Antão, there was hardly any wind. The sky was cloudy, but the full moon provided plenty of light and we secured the wheel for a quiet night. The next day the wind returned along with a choppy and wild sea. Unpredictable wind patterns continued to dominate our days.

> *Kee: Life on board continued to be full of surprises. At one point, Björn dived overboard, fully clothed, to rescue insurance documents that had fallen into the sea, forcing us to quickly adjust our direction to pick him up. When the weather was quiet, Fons and Frank climbed into their diving gear and jumped into the clear water, holding on to the floating rope attached to the ship. I didn't dare join them in the deep. It was around 5,000 metres and sharks*

could attack at any moment. I watched their movements from the underwater observatory and kept an eye on the surroundings. When they were back on board, I swam around Seaview in goggles and a snorkel. Fons and I liked to sit in the underwater compartment, looking at life below us: tiny triggerfish, small mackerel, and many plankton. We found ourselves discussing the idea of children and I realised I liked the idea.

Despite the usual leaks and broken equipment, Fons kept our unique ship functional through all manner of repairs. The crew's ingenuity always won through. Frank sawed through a drum and made it into a barbecue, using my iron bicycle basket as a grill. Fons built an underwater case for his camera, testing it by letting it drop down into the sea on a

The view from the Seaview's observation chamber

15-metre line. It turned out to be completely waterproof. He made beautiful recordings of the ship's underside and the boys who were frolicking around in the water. It was sweltering, and we were incredibly slow. A southeasterly wind came. The sails were billowing starboard. We could swim along after Seaview *without effort because the ship sucked us along. A school of silver-coloured fish was swimming under us, but we did not understand why there were no dorados when we saw the flying fish chasing around. We missed the dorado. Why did we hardly see them here? Were they afraid of this strange-shaped ship?*

Early one morning, we heard a "tock tock" noise against the hull in our cabins, as though someone was hitting it with a small hammer. This was followed by heavy breathing. Up ahead, we saw the gigantic back and fins of a whale. He was sending the tock signals out to investigate what type of being we were and if we could become friends. We jumped into the water, hoping that he would come closer, but he did not. However, when we were back on board, he did approach, and we saw that he was about 15 metres long.

Björn shouted from the top of the mast when the whale surfaced, so that we could take some good pictures. He was too far from our underwater observatory to take photos there. We remained very excited during the whale's time with us. It was overwhelming and touching that this primal animal of the ocean sought contact with us. Slowly, the whale moved on, but we kept hearing his signals inside against the steel wall for quite a while. And then, in his wake, we saw pretty green and blue dorado around us.

We were not moving along our course fast enough. At night we shuffled back and forth between the steering wheel and the genoa to get onto the right course, and in three days, we had only gone 55 miles to the west. Our route zigzagged considerably and sometimes even turned back upon itself. The distance we had covered by boat in 24 hours, we could have walked in three hours. Fortunately, the dorados played around us, keeping spirits high.

Having covered 1,100 nautical miles from Cabo Verde and with 1,000 still to go to Barbados, our days were full of swimming, radio communications and games of chess. When I fixed Björn's tape recorder, we also had music on deck for the first time. Radio communication with the mainland made us feel closer to home; chats with fellow Norwegians were important to Björn, giving him a sense of connection. The sight of a ship in the distance was another reminder that there were still other people on Earth.

> *Kee: One night, during my watch, I lost control of the wheel and went completely off course.* Seaview *was suddenly lying sideways and I couldn't manoeuvre her back on track. When I woke Fons, he said that I would have to try and sort it out myself. When he eventually came to help, he simply switched on the engine and took the ship back on course. Such a simple solution had never occurred to me! As the voyage continued, we all grew, not just as sailors, but also as problem-solvers, learning to handle situations we had never faced before. On 22 March, our morale soared as we crossed the 50th meridian west. We threw a message in a bottle into the sea, offering $20 to the finder.*

We started receiving signals from Radio Barbados and learnt that a light aircraft would be flying out to greet us. In the meantime, we swayed terribly. The high seas hurled the soup Kee was making out of the pot. Breakfast rolled around the floor. Our jar of instant coffee emptied itself in the cupboard, and a crack appeared in the oil bottle, which leaked everywhere until it was empty. After the pan of rice fell onto the ground, I told Kee it would be best if she stopped cooking and we just ate cold things out of cans. It was proving a tough home stretch.

I stretched a line from the radio aerial to the top of the mast to try out the 40-metre band. It did not work, but I did manage to talk on the 15-metre band. Barbados came through loud and clear. That was not surprising since we were only one degree to the east of them. We saw a large bird gliding down to pluck a fish from the sea beside us – the land had to be close by. Hours later, local fishing boats appeared and we followed their course. The aircraft appeared above us at sunset, and darkness brought the lights of Barbados! We had been on the ocean for 50 days since Cabo Verde.

We only saw Barbados when we were very close since the island is low lying. We spotted boats arrive in the distance. To our amusement, the officials ordered us to remove the frigate bird sitting in the mast before we could moor; we were not allowed to 'bring the animal into the country' because of possible disease. Björn got rid of the bird, but after a few wing strokes it returned to sit on *Seaview*. However, now it was okay as it had come on board in Barbados this time!

Björn and Frank left us on a huge luxury yacht bound for Antigua. Unfortunately, the ship sank on the reef just before the coast, but luckily the crew were saved by helicopters. Frank returned to Oslo and Björn went off to America, where he met some fellow Norwegians building an original Viking ship and decided to help them.

Seaview became a local attraction and tourist boats changed their course to pass. We offered to donate her to the government because they planned to create an underwater park, but, frustratingly, while Barbados officials seemed pleased, they said they would need six months to decide. That was too long to wait and we became increasingly at peace with the idea of scuttling her. The idea was to complete our adventure by letting our unique ship sink into deep water eight miles west of Barbados, where she would pose no danger to shipping. It had to be a worthy end for the vessel, which had been our home and slow means of transport for so long.

So five weeks after our arrival, *Countrygirl* followed us out to take us on board later. There was also a photographer from the *Daily Nation* newspaper onboard. Scuttling our beloved *Seaview* was the end of the project and something we had to capture on film.

We opened the sea cocks and used a heavy hammer to smash the portholes of the cabins. When they reached water level, the ship would fill up and disappear under the waves. I thought that

Seaview *going down*

this would take at least an hour. Calmly, Kee and I descended into all the cabins to say goodbye to our home of many months. Our certainty that we had plenty of time was rudely interrupted by panicked shouts. 'Quick! Leave the ship!'

The water had already reached the portholes, and thousands of litres were pouring in. *Seaview* pitched sternwards. The deck was already disappearing under the waves. Kee slid across the sloping deck with all the cameras around her neck and jumped for the rubber boat, while I cut the line loose at the very last moment. Together with the pitching and sinking *Seaview*, we disappeared under the waves.

Desperately I cast around and managed to catch the rope around the small dinghy to hold on to it and pull myself up. With awe-inspiring foaming and booming, the prow reared up, and *Seaview* disappeared, roaring and gargling under the waves, as she headed towards the seabed nearly 1,800 metres below us. The thick steel mast with full sails narrowly passed us as it fell with a big smack into the sea. In the foaming white mass of waves around us, bits and pieces were floating everywhere.

And then all went quiet.

Everything had happened in the space of a few minutes. We barely had time to realise the danger we were in, before our great orange lifebuoy shot from the depths at tremendous speed. We trembled as we watched the bizarre spectacle in disbelief and dismay. The shocked photographer had only been able to take two photos, both at an angle. We failed to record anything and were lucky our cameras were still intact. Unable to speak, we sailed back to Barbados in silence. A remarkable end to our remarkable *Seaview*. The next day a leading article in the *Daily Nation* led with 'That Sinking Feeling'.

Mechanical Mayhem
Floating Truck

Two years had passed since our *Seaview* expedition. It had been a bittersweet time. My father had tragically lost his life after falling from his dovecote and breaking his ribs, and Kee had discovered she was pregnant on the same morning. Despite complications during childbirth, our son Robin was born on June 30, 1982, bringing hope amidst the sorrow.

By then, I was working in truck maintenance. These vehicles and their engines were remarkable: they were solidly constructed, reliable and showed well thought out mechanics. 'These trucks are amazing – you could drive one across the Atlantic,' I casually remarked one day. 'Oh, yes?' came the retort. 'Then why don't you?!'

So I set out to do just that. The idea of driving a truck across the Atlantic Ocean from New York to Lisbon was born. I was sure the engine and the truck would be able to withstand the harsh circumstances of an ocean crossing.

It was December 1982. In contrast to the ten-year project of constructing *Seaview*, I intended to complete the construction of this vessel in just four months. First and foremost, I had to have a floating structure of two large, cylinder-shaped tanks which would be divided into compartments to hold fuel, water and supplies. Then I needed a truck as reliable as those I had worked on and a Perkins diesel engine. After many technical calculations, I concluded that a truck of about six tonnes would be the most appropriate to function as a living space, wheelhouse and engine room. It would never have an ideal streamline, but that didn't really matter. The vehicle's existing engine would have to drive a propeller using its gearbox and driveshaft. I did not want to change anything more than I had to on the truck, to keep it original.

A metalworks company informed us they could supply pipes to comply with my specifications. These were sections for a chimney destined for an aluminium factory in South Africa, but the company cancelled that project. The eight-metre-long cylinders had a diameter of one and a half metres. The metal was half a centimetre thick. They were exactly what I needed as flotation for the raft and would provide fuel tanks and storage. I created ten compartments by welding in bulkheads. Six of them would be tanks to hold diesel oil.

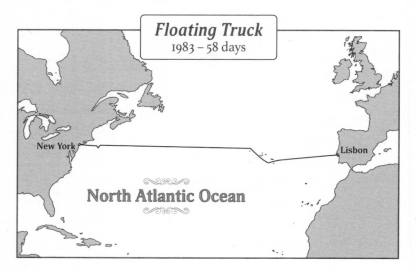

Floating Truck
1983 – 58 days

New York — Lisbon

North Atlantic Ocean

There was good news. Van Gend & Loos, a large transport company, was willing to make one of their trucks available to us. Although initially deeming us utterly crazy, the director's enthusiasm grew once I had convinced him I knew what I was talking about, leading to his complete faith in our endeavour.

I selected an eight-tonne Dodge truck with a closed steel load compartment, a thick wooden floor and aluminium plating on the outside. The roof consisted of solid and transparent plates made from synthetic material. On the back, two large doors that could be opened individually would provide ample access for materials and crew. The engine had a capacity of 120 horsepower. One disadvantage was that the cab had to be tipped forward to reach the engine underneath. On land, that was an advantage, but at sea, the continuous swell might make this a problem. The engine, propeller and drive system had to be technically sound. We assumed we would have to drive the truck day and night across the Atlantic Ocean for more than two months, sometimes in harsh conditions.

Launch day was also construction day; we still had to secure the propeller to the axle. There was excitement in the air as our eyes followed the tubular frame, gliding through the air on taut cables before being lowered onto the water. The wires were slackened until the whole thing was floating. The waterline was still far too high, but should, all being well, touch the water when the truck was lowered onto the frame. Minutes later, the truck was dangling above the tubes, and it all came together perfectly, precisely on the waterline. Everyone applauded. We held the christening ceremony with two bottles: one containing Dutch milk and the other Belgian beer. With the words: 'We christen you *Floating Truck* and wish you safe sailing. May you be protected until you return home.' Kee swung the bottles against the bow, where they smashed, spraying milk and foaming beer everywhere.

The voyage was to be from New York to Lisbon, and our vessel, already loaded onto a trailer, was driven into the Polish ship, *Wladislaw Sikorski*. I say "driven" because the new 200-metre-long French-built vessel was known as a ConRo, a hybrid ship that had roll-on roll-off facilities below deck but was also able to carry containers on deck. So, rather than being hoisted onto the ship's upper deck, *Floating Truck* was driven into the below-deck area through her giant stern door.

Meanwhile, we took the plane to JFK.

The day before we left for New York, we took Robin to my mother in her village in the north of Belgium. There was no doubt in our minds that he would be well cared for. Our hearts ached at leaving him for so long, but it was for the best. Kee wanted to put him to bed herself that evening and held him

After launch Floating Truck *enroute to harbour for shipping*

close until he was almost asleep. She cut off a lock of his blond hair and placed it in a locket, together with his recent photos. Our friends, Marion and Michel, would pick him up there and bring him to Lisbon when we arrived with the truck. A lot would be happening between now and then.

The low loader carrying our *Floating Truck* was unloaded at Port Newark and parked in the container area from where a crane swung our vessel across the harbour water. We were afloat once again and as Americans say, we needed to gas up. The harbour master recommended we motor out 15 miles past Coney Island and into Sheepshead Bay off South Brooklyn to do so. From driving tests in Rotterdam I had carefully calculated we needed 7,300 litres diesel to get us across the Atlantic to Lisbon. We filled up our tanks with 2,000 US gallons, just over 7,500 litres.

*

We had been waiting for this moment for months. People were waving us off from a flotilla of boats. As soon as we got to Rockaway Point, we felt the full force of the open Atlantic. In the shallow waters, high, short waves smashed onto the wheelhouse with thunderous brutality, and it felt like we were repeatedly diving into a deep well. We could hardly stay in our seats, and Kee was afraid the truck would break off the floaters. I assured her that was impossible and lowered the engine's rpm to 1,200, after which the jolts subsided slightly.

Darkness fell quickly and New York's glow illuminated the skyline behind us. Thousands of lights shone on Staten Island and Long Island, but toward the south-east, the chilly dark mouth of the Northern Atlantic Ocean gaped. We intended to keep a southeasterly course until we came under the 40th latitude and then follow that. The island of Flores in the Azores and Lisbon, our final destination, were both approximately on the 39th latitude. The weather service called the first hurricane warnings the week before our departure. We would be sailing through the areas described as "danger zones" during these months.

That first night we plodded along restlessly, always on guard in case we met any ships, even though our planned southern course would soon take us away from the major shipping routes. By dawn, we had lost sight of land. The water was grey and dark; we were probably still in relatively shallow waters of less than 200 metres. Seventy miles south-east of New York, there are occasional spots with a depth of only 15 metres, but after that, the ocean soon drops to a depth of 2,750 metres. Behind us, a shark fin slid through the water, making us uneasy. In these much colder North Atlantic waters, we did not expect many of them.

*

It was 6pm and misty when Kee shouted that a ship was approaching us. I saw a long cannon which suggested this was a navy vessel. I tuned the marine telephone to the international communication channel 16, and we were informed that we were dealing with the United States Coastguard and must switch to channel 14. The crew had seen a bizarre, slow-moving contact on their radar screen, and an alert had been sent out. There had even been speculation that it was the conning tower of a Russian submarine. To their surprise, a floating truck had then been spotted. They asked our permission to come on board, and an inflatable manned by six men in combat suits began racing towards us. While one crew member circled *Floating Truck* in their huge dinghy, the others politely introduced themselves.

Their surprise grew as they saw the construction and learnt about our plans to travel to Europe. They thought we intended

Floating Truck | *Twin floats on the road to join up with the Dodge truck.*

Floating Truck | *Family breakfast aboard the Dodge truck before it leaves for New York.*

Floating Truck | *Steady motoring eastwards towards Flores in the Azores.*

Floating Truck | *Stern view with the gas cylinder soon to create the inferno.*

Floating Truck | *Kee washing after trucker's lunch.*

Floating Truck | *Recovering in the Azores.*

Floating Truck | *Berthed at Lisbon*

Flying Bottle | *Work on Detroit diesel and hydraulic equipment.*

Flying Bottle | *Test flight for hydrofoil near Amsterdam.*

Flying Bottle | *The 1,000 HP Detroit diesel and hydraulic equipment.*

Flying Bottle | *Brothers Robin and Brendan on board.*

Flying Bottle | *Final touches to new livery.*

Message in a Bottle | *Fons and Kee in the Canaries.*

Message in a Bottle | *Departing Cabo Verde.*

Message in a Bottle | *At home in the saloon.*

Message in a Bottle | *Under sail in a westerly wind to Barbados.*

to sail along the American coast, at most, but had gone in the wrong direction. The mothership captain asked his officer to check we had sufficient fuel and rescue equipment on board. When that turned out to be in order, they asked us to send a message upon arriving in Europe. Fortunately, we remembered to ask for our position: 39° 51' N 72° 39' W. So, we were located just under the 40th latitude and almost 90 nautical miles from New York. Perfect. This meant we had sailed nearly four knots despite our slow progress for the first 12 hours due to headwinds and heavy seas. The coastguard gave three long whistles before heading northwards. I depressed the clutch, put the truck in fourth gear and automatically switched the right indicator while turning the wheel towards the eastern horizon.

*

Our mechanical engineering challenges began. When there was a headwind, spray passed through the radiator, lowering the engine temperature worryingly. Once in a while, the instrument only showed 50°C, which was harmful to the pistons and cylinders, causing rapid corrosion. To reduce the cooling, I decided to protect the radiator in part with a panel. We were pleased to see the needle rise to 70°C.

The wind turned northerly, and within a few hours, the waves came directly from the port side, which led to annoying swaying and pounding movements. Kee began to be sick, and this continued all night. She had to throw up from the cab window when she sat behind the wheel. It generally landed on the door and was washed off by the splashing seawater. Wretched for her. I sat in the cab as much as possible to give her some rest. Being seasick is exhausting. Kee did not take any medicine; she said that her body had to get accustomed to the sea by itself. That could take up to 42 days.

At 3am, the dashboard lights suddenly lost intensity. The batteries were almost empty, which could only be caused by a malfunctioning alternator. I turned off the power-draining navigation lights to ensure the batteries kept enough electricity for the instrument lighting. We were now just a dark shadow riding the waves, so panic set in when we spotted a ship approaching us. We saw the port and starboard navigation lights with a dancing white top light between them. They were heading right for us. I lit the oil lamps and placed them starboard while Kee redirected our course to 90 degrees portside. The vessel was a fishing boat, which reduced speed and let us pass. I would have to look into what was happening when daylight came, but I assumed we needed our spare alternator.

More problems followed. The continuous day and night steering was already exhausting, and now the compass light had stopped working, so we had to shine a torch onto the instrument throughout the night. Once or twice, the simultaneous shining, peering and steering caused us to turn full circle before getting us back on our easterly course. I regretted not having mounted a rudder angle indicator. We now had to study the compass almost continuously.

I also had to calculate precisely how much fuel we used in one day. I descended into the starboard flotation chamber through the forward hatch and assessed the liquid level in the gauge glass. It was alarmingly low. After using several methods to calculate the volume, I concluded to my horror that we had consumed nearly 200 litres in the last 24 hours. If that were to continue, we would only have enough for 35 days, which might not even get us to the Azores. Kee became desperate when I told her that we would probably end up without any power, 300 miles west of the closest land. I had to find a solution. Our only option was to reduce the engine speed from 1,500 to 1,200 rpm. That was when the engine was most efficient and used the least fuel. However, I had to ensure the speed reduction did not cancel out the fuel-saving. I let the rev counter fall back three stripes.

We decided we were probably at the Sargasso Sea's edge since we frequently passed vast fields of Sargasso seaweed. Sometimes the strands were up to 50 metres long. Initially, we tried to circumvent the plants but soon discovered they did not harm our propeller.

A beaming sun glowed above the eastern horizon, and the wind was force 5 due west. I was short of breath and suffered from a tight chest, caused by the poisonous exhaust fumes from the generator I used to recharge the batteries. The fumes blew inside while I was sleeping in the cargo box. Dizziness and a splitting headache made it impossible for me to do any decent thinking. Kee felt awful too.

Unlike my previous rafts, *Floating Truck*'s deck was usually sopping wet. The water disappeared between the planks, but the spray penetrated everything. I was happy to sit in the relatively dry driver's cab, whereas Kee preferred steering with a tiller in the open air, as we had done on the raft. As yet, we had made no duty schedule but took over the steering wheel whenever convenient. There were never more than two hours between shifts, not even at night.

We often had to go outside and crank the large lubricator's handle to grease the bearings of the propeller shaft. One evening, I heard the driveshaft, or maybe the prop shaft, making a sinister noise. I was afraid that the axle's thrust bearing had given up the ghost and that it was just a question of time before we had irreparable damage. I regularly looked between the raft floaters, shining a torch to see if any irregularities appeared in the propulsion. Everything seemed normal. The drive shafts were continuously engulfed by the sea, so I could hardly make them out. We would just have to wait and see.

> **Kee:** *Fons's shortness of breath soon passed. He was always active, keeping the engine under control, lubricating the axles, turning the fuel tanks on or off, or studying the sea charts. I admired him. One evening, Fons told me he was afraid the prop shaft would give out. Something like that was impossible to repair. At times, I felt paralysed with fear and despair. When would we be able to see Robin again? We talked about what we would do if we broke down. There was not a ship in sight. When I lay in my bed later, I could not sleep. I was trembling as I lay there, listening to the thumping. I begged from the bottom of my heart for us to reach the Azores. Every five minutes, Fons disappeared under* Floating Truck *with a torch. I just felt miserable. Fons made me rest and let me sleep for a long time. I only steered from half past midnight to 3.30am, and he carried on until I finally woke up at 8am, feeling much better.*

Day 5. Beautiful clear weather, but the beneficial west wind had disappeared. Strangely enough, Kee was feeling very good. I took the engine to 1,500 rpm for a bit, at which point the strange noise in the propulsion disappeared. That meant it was not the prop shaft thumping. It was the driveshaft, which could not harm the bearings, so I could lower the rpm again. This went well. When we measured our location, it indicated that we had hardly reduced our speed now that the propeller was turning more slowly.

In the evening, the compass lighting stopped working again. The water, which continued to splash over us, could not get into the compass casing, but the lamps and electric wiring to the driver's cab suffered from the corrosive salt. It was cold and wet as I fixed the wiring. I lost a small screwdriver, despite being very careful with my irreplaceable tools. The lighting disappeared no less than five times. When the illumination packed in completely, Kee put the hurricane lamp behind the windscreen. In its flickering glow, we could barely see the triangle that represented due east on the compass. Steering was so tiring that we sat behind the wheel, nodding off. That night we saw no lights that might have indicated a ship's presence. The oppressive desolation of the ocean had us in its grip.

The six fuel tanks built into the raft floats manually fed the trucks fuel tank and I realised the truck's own fuel tank must be almost empty. If the engine ran out of fuel, the whole system would have to be vented. Plus, it took a lot of power to restart the engine. Unfortunately, I was too late and the engine stalled with a splutter. For the first time, we had to lift and open the heavy tilt cab at sea. That took work. Positioned on either side, we waited for precisely the right time within the wave pattern and tried to push the heavy cab up. If that did not work, it fell back, and we had to be quick to get out of its way. When we had finally tilted the cab, I checked all cables, the oil level and the radiator. It was also time to fit a new alternator. The old one was destroyed, and even the heavy connectors for the wires had been damaged by electrolysis.

I had worked with engines hundreds of times before, but this was different. I had to be careful that the screws I loosened didn't fall into the sea. The pounding and rolling truck made it difficult to keep the parts in the right place, but I screwed all the bolts tight while the saltwater ran over the engine. The fully charged batteries allowed us to use the automatic pilot again. After venting the six injectors, we let the cab fall shut.

To our dismay, we saw that the aerial for the marine telephone lay broken on the cab's roof. The metre-long tube had knocked against the mast when we tilted the driver's cab and the impact had shattered the casing. Without the aerial, we couldn't talk to other ships or the coastguard when we approached land. Kee gave me Robin's wooden toy cart for the repairs, and I sawed off a piece and attached it to the aerial antenna using Sellotape. We would have to wait until we saw another ship to test whether the radio would work.

We started the engine again. The alternator worked perfectly and charged the battery immediately. We could turn on the autopilot again and felt very spoilt that we could now do something other than steer. Despite our best efforts, the automatic pilot provided a more stable course than we could maintain at the helm. We hoped this meant the enormous zigzagging of the last few days was over; otherwise, we would not have enough fuel.

We expected to have drifted even further towards the south. However, the navigation figures showed we were exactly on

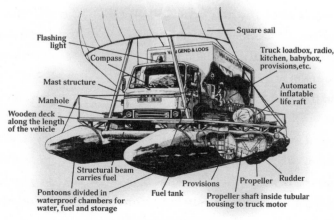

Newspaper drawing of Floating Truck

course on the 40th latitude. The longitude was 63° 46'. We had covered 150 nautical miles in one day. We never again equalled that distance or speed. We kept our northeasterly course for another day to prevent us from drifting further south. According to the pilot chart, we did not seem to have entered the favourable northeasterly currents with their speed of one knot in August. The long strands of Sargasso seaweed were drifting on an east-west line, which helped us assess the currents' direction. We were just 14 miles further south than yesterday and had covered 130 miles in 24 hours. According to the pilot chart, there was only a six per cent chance of an easterly wind this month, and we got it.

*

The wind turned due east, the worst direction for us, and we were rocking terribly. The waves smashed against the driver's cab with thunderous roars. The sea exploded against the windscreen threatening to blow out the glass with its enormous force, alarming us both by distorting the glass more than a centimetre inward. A shattered windscreen could prove fatal. On top of this, the engine's temperature dropped to an unacceptable level. I glanced into the engine room and saw a wet, foaming mass. A well-sealed diesel engine is resilient as long as the intake sucks in no water. I was surprised the engine never complained, despite being practically submerged. With difficulty, I placed a wooden board under the engine, covering the holes that let the cooling air flow to the radiator so that the radiator sucked in much less water. The engine temperature went up 15°C.

It was annoying that we were getting exhaust fumes in the cargo box when there was a headwind. The slipstream effects behind the truck were to blame. Strangely, we had no problems when the wind came from behind, considering the rudder was where the fumes rose from the water.

> *Kee: This was the riskiest project we had ever done. If there was a technical malfunction, we were doomed since the winds and currents were not such that we would reach the other side. On* Last Generation *and* Seaview, *the risk of technical problems was much smaller, and we had generally been sailing in beneficial currents and winds. Everything was jumbled up this time. The wind kept coming from the east, and the constant spray of water made us feel cold and miserable. The only time I felt safe was lying in our bunk with my body against Fons under the sleeping bag.*

We were sitting outside *Floating Truck* on the life raft eating our meal when the sun suddenly disappeared behind the cargo box and reappeared on the other side. The waves washed across us and made a mess of our food. We were spinning around! The thought, 'The rudder is broken,' flashed through my mind. We ran to the cab. The steering wheel had entirely turned towards starboard and was held in place by the automatic pilot. After switching it off, I was able to turn the wheel to the middle, and the truck returned to our rightful course. What was going on?

I pressed the start button of the instrument again, but the wheel kept turning starboard. Our automatic pilot was no longer working, meaning we had to go back to manual steering, I realised in shock. To make matters worse, the voltmeter showed a very low battery voltage which meant no charge current. Had the new alternator already given up? Or was something wrong with the wiring? The reason was probably the awful humidity, which had soaked everything for days and caused short circuits. Maybe we could do something to fix it, but first, everything had to be dry. Our meals together were over. Things were about to become very heavy and tiring again. Flores was still 1,250 miles away.

With our batteries nearly empty, we could rarely switch on the windscreen wipers, just when we needed them most, with water incessantly spraying over the windshield. When I took over the watch from Kee, she was exhausted and her eyes hurt from staring at the half-lit compass. During the last hour of my watch, I started nodding off. When Kee took over from me at 1am, she saw a ship portside and managed to hold a steady course for three hours, but she told me later that it had been a challenge as the wind strengthened. She was terrified that the crashing waves would smash the windshield. There was no point in sailing any further. We hardly moved forward, and it had become physically too strenuous. We were better off waiting until the solid easterly wind subsided. I stopped the engine and threw the sea anchor off the stern.

> *Kee: The sea anchor was useless. We were sailing backwards. I found myself yelling at the high, grey waves that came charging towards us, continuing to push us back. 'Get lost, you bastards. Leave us alone!' The wind did not diminish for seven hours, so Fons decided to motor again. Once again, we were smashing against the waves.*
>
> *Steering in this wretchedly strong headwind wore us out, and my arm muscles were in constant pain. The wind finally subsided when the sun was almost on the horizon. I hardly dared to believe it. Fons discovered that the protective board under the engine had come loose. He wanted to fix it straight away, as it might otherwise break. Seeing Fons balancing on small protrusions, half beneath the engine, above nearly 3,000 metres of water was scary. I was terrified he would slip into the sea, and afraid I*

would not have enough strength to catch him if anything went wrong. Luckily, Fons managed to fix everything in half an hour.

Since our fuel consumption made us lighter, the exhaust rose above the water more often, blowing its nauseating gases into our living room. Unfortunately, we could not make a ventilation hole in the roof. It made me sick, but Fons still managed his coffee and crackers.

We spotted a drifting red and white buoy bobbing near us and Fons wanted to pick it up. It had a radar reflector and carried the marking 'Lady Clare', probably from a fishing boat. With me at the steering wheel, Fons yelled instructions to approach it, telling me to keep clear of its trailing lines. It was not easy. After he managed to fish it out and get back in the cab, he made a sarcastic remark, saying that he would never dare to be a passenger in a vehicle I drove on land. I reminded him that I did not have a driving licence anyway.

I wanted to tow the abandoned buoy behind us as a rescue aid in case one of us fell overboard. But I had to abandon the plan because the buoy's resistance could increase fuel consumption. We had now covered almost 1,000 miles without the usual rescue line trailing behind us. On deck, there was one primitive railing, consisting of a rope stretched around it at the height of one metre. We were better off reinforcing the railing by adding another cord to it. The chances were high that the truck's engine noise would drown out the sound of either of us crying for help in an emergency, and I scared myself, imagining Kee not turning up to relieve me at the end of my watch.

We were anxious about bad weather approaching us in September. The pilot chart of August indicated that icebergs had been spotted in this area several times before. My fears about the alternator and the wiring came true. Corrosion and electrolysis had left them damaged beyond repair. I could not remove the alternator because it also kept the water pump's V-belt tight. Our electricity supply was now wholly reliant on our little power generator, which had to keep recharging the batteries. Fortunately, I had brought extra petrol. The now-essential machine had problems starting and also made an ominous ticking sound.

Trucks are designed for use on land, and here in the Atlantic, *Floating Truck*'s electricals were only partially protected. They are not meant to deal with frequent and furious onslaughts of seawater. It wouldn't have been hard to build protection all around the truck and adapt all manner of things, but my aim was to drive across the Atlantic Ocean in an original truck. The only changes I found acceptable were securing the vehicle on the floats which also served as fuel tanks, joining the prop shaft to the propeller axle and fixing the rudder auto steering equipment. The rest had to remain unchanged.

It always annoys me immensely when people undertake so-called brave and risky endeavours but forget to tell you that a supporting film crew or boat is on hand at all times. Knowing we were truly isolated and far removed from any real help was a mental burden that weighed heavily on the whole undertaking. I would not have been lying awake for nights trying to figure out construction details about the truck's optimal seaworthiness if I knew there was an accompanying ship nearby. Many documentaries give a distorted view of events since the solo polar or jungle explorer is always beautifully filmed and is accompanied by a camera crew who often reach the peak or pole long before them.

Kee: Sometimes, during my watch at night, I felt so tired that it seemed as if my heart was too weary to continue beating. Fons felt terrible for me, but he had no energy left either. I hardly went outside. When Fons was doing repairs, I had to steer for hours on end. I always kept an eye on Fons in the rearview mirror. He often balanced dangerously on the edge of the deck, and I was petrified every time he disappeared out of my sight. One time, in a panic, I let go of the steering wheel, jumped out of the cab and found him peeing behind the one shut door of the cargo box, the one place I had no visibility of. I was so happy I had asked him to make those little windows in the cargo box so that we could keep an eye on each other and signal to one another.

The engine was not using much lubricating oil despite running day and night. The cylinder block was completely crusted in salt. But I was worried about the radiator. Salt covered the thin cooling pipes and if they got damaged, we would lose cooling fluid. Although I had brought a solder and blowtorch, repairing the radiator would be difficult on board.

On one of our most challenging nights, the engine stalled. I assumed it was another clogged-up fuel filter. But, at first sight, the oil tubes and filters appeared to be in order. My next thought was that the pump could no longer suck fuel from the middle chambers on the floats because the level had become too low. I was right, and after I connected the truck fuel tank again, the engine started immediately. But after driving for an hour, the engine stalled again. This time, the filter was blocked. A black substance shot into my nose and moustache as I blew through it. We had no choice but to blow through our two remaining filters every time the engine stalled.

We felt the wind waking up. It settled in the south-west, ideal for us, although soon foaming breakers played across the choppy sea, making it more burdensome and tiring to steer. The air became threatening and dark. The blue gave way to fickle jet-black masses of windswept clouds. There was a storm on the way! Probably an offshoot from a Caribbean hurricane that was about to steamroll over us. The ocean's hellish racket was amplified in *Floating Truck*'s cargo-living box, making it impossible to stay there. I shut and locked the large doors. We both had to remain alert and sit together in the driver's cab. Alternately, we lay down on the seat in a distorted position to grab some rest while the other wrestled the wheel like a possessed rally driver. Heavy rain showers made it impossible for us to see the compass. Staying balanced on the seat was extremely difficult, so we had to seek support by grasping any part of the truck we could. The howling wind was still gathering strength and kept stirring up masses of water. We managed to stay in front of the wind and slid wildly into the valleys between the waves, only to be smashed down somewhere else a little later, as if by the hand of a giant.

I switched the marine telephone to channel 16. A passing ship was already trying to contact us. They let us know we were experiencing storm force 10 conditions and gave us our location. By dawn conditions had not improved. Huge waves lifted our buoyancy hulls and dragged the vehicle along with them only to drop into the swirling valley of the next wave. I had extended the air intake tube to protrude 30 centimetres above the truck's roof, about three and a half metres above the waterline. But in these conditions, I was worried spray and water would be sucked in and degrade the lubricating oil. All our muscles were hurting and bruises kept appearing from heavy contact and abrasions. The wind was increasing again. Suddenly the engine noise fell away, and we heard only the sea's roar. We looked at each other desperately. The truck was out of control and fell into the clutches of the waves. Despairing, we jumped out of the cab. The terrible swaying threw everything in the cargo box back and forth. Fortunately, the fuel filter and the wiring were now located on the windward side, so it might be possible to track down the fault.

I was alarmed to see the glass pot of the water separator full of seawater – that meant water had reached one of the containers, which could have fatal consequences for the engine's fragile fuel pump. The whole fuel system had to be rinsed with clean oil to remove the water. Tilting the cab had become very dangerous, but we managed it with a lot of effort. The microfilter housing was also full of water, as were the tubes and the pump. Seawater rippled around the engine and made the task of dismounting the parts hazardous. But eventually, I could pump the whole system through until we had clean fuel from the pipes. As long as the fuel pump was not damaged, the engine should be able to run.

There was no time to catch our breath. If we started the engine to correct our orientation to the wind, an enormous wave could capsize us, but we had to try. The engine stuttered as we turned the key, but it didn't start. We had to make it run before the batteries ran empty, or the consequences would be dramatic. On our fourth attempt, the engine started. We were tired, wet and filthy but relieved as we sheltered in the soaked cab. Our living space had become uninhabitable. Everything was soaked and scattered about: mattresses, clothes, food and books. We squinted between the horizontal rain showers for any other ships. Our white-grey superstructure would be hard to spot now everything around us was the same colour, and ocean vessels do not always have their radar systems switched on.

We motored for nearly an hour before the engine stuttered and fell silent again. This time there was no water in the fuel lines. I suspected a problem with the microfilter. It took a superhuman effort to tilt the cab. I replaced the filter with our last spare and ventilated the fuel system between the waves flooding us. After that, the engine ran perfectly again. Hours later, to our relief, we could feel the strong winds subsiding. We later discovered that a violent offshoot from Hurricane Alicia had attacked us.

*

Around this time, we encountered another problem with the generator refusing to work. I used it to recharge the batteries every time they were empty from restarting the engine. The driving rain had made the ignition mechanism so wet that it no longer generated high voltage. I decided to wait before I dismounted the part. There was a good chance that the moisture would disappear by itself. It would be a disaster if the batteries got too weak to start the engine repeatedly.

Since I could not find any defects in the fuel pipes, I removed the fuel pump. It looked perfect and hardly contained any dirt. The engine started at the first attempt, and this time it kept running. After an hour, however, we were lying still again. It turned out that the inlet pipe was sucked shut so the oil could not get through the lines. Loosening the plastic pipe and securing it again solved the problem for another hour. That afternoon it happened another four times.

I had not expected this type of problem. To top it all off, I dropped a vital piece of copper tubing through the deck and into the sea. I had to cut one out in a different place to replace it. Kee shone the torch all the time so that I could work. Taking time to rest was out of the question these days. The compass light also failed again later that day. The wire had broken. The generator would no longer start. After some tinkering, I was lucky to get it working. And so, it continued night and day. We were utterly exhausted and despondent.

> *Kee: Day 17 was the worst so far. The variable, inconsistent wind on our side made steering heavy. I would have big biceps by the time we arrived in Lisbon. We scooped oil from the central tanks into all the cans and pans we could find and then manoeuvred carefully to empty the tanks at the stern. Because of the sudden and violent jolts, it was a slow and fumbling process. Some of the oil landed on the deck and ended up in the sea. An imaginary passer-by would have watched in amazement as the bedraggled man and woman repeatedly ran back and forth with objects on a couple of planks around a truck. We stank of diesel oil since we had to suck on the plastic tube to siphon it.*

Dirt often blocked the sieve in the too-small funnel. The centre starboard tank's fuel was less dirty, although the tank had an identical rubber covering to the backboard tank. I could think of no explanation for this. We were desperate because of the time lost scooping and pouring fuel between the tanks. But the solution to the problem of manually shuttling fuel turned out to be so simple that I could have kicked myself for not thinking of it earlier. My exhaustion meant that I could not always think clearly. By using our gas bottle I was able put pressure into the dirty diesel tanks. And then I connected the centre tanks to the stern tanks. Automatically and quickly, our two stern tanks filled up. Not a drop was lost. Now we just had to wait to see what would happen with the filters containing the mix of clean and dirty oil. To be safe, we blew these parts clean before going on our way again. We cheered at our latitude, which turned out to be 41° 37'. Only 500 nautical miles left to Flores! Maybe we would make it.

> *Kee: The engine soon fell silent, suggesting the filters were completely clogged up. What would we do without filters? We started to think about ways to make our own. We pulled one of the filters apart so that only the frame was left. I fished what I considered suitable material from my rag bag and wound it around the filter frame. But Fons preferred my lingerie as a filter because it was gauzier. He tied it down securely using pieces of string.*

At 5.30am, the engine started without problems. Only the fuel filter continued to taunt us. One last possibility was the water separator, which contained no sieve or filter. Kee had asked me to dismantle it several times, and this time I did. To my surprise, a tiny sieve was hidden from sight and filled with dirt. And that was it! All those nights of misery could largely be attributed to this minor component, which could so easily be cleaned. We hardly dared believe we were now freed from our fuel problems.

And yet, the truck had hardly gone into the pitch-black night when the engine began to run faster, and then eventually stopped. All it could be was the microfilter being full of dirt. Cab up, filter tube disconnected, element blown through using our cooking gas bottle, fuel system ventilated. By now, it had become a tiresome routine. To blow the filter clean for the umpteenth time, Kee brought the gas bottle to the door and opened the gas while I held the gas tube against the filter on the stern deck blowing black oil and dirt in all directions.

With our reduced thinking capacity, we had entirely forgotten the flickering storm lamp on the floor of the cargo box in our makeshift living space. A sudden gust of wind blew the gas towards the oil lamp. There was a deafening explosion and huge flames, with Kee at the centre.

After the Bang

Floating Truck

Kee cried out in pain, terrified the flames had burnt her face. Reflexively, I turned off the gas, and as the fire died down I grabbed the jerrycan and doused us with water. Not knowing how badly we were burnt or where the burns were, I dived into our 'cellar' to tear open milk cartons and throw them over Kee. She had no eyebrows or eyelashes left and was afraid her face would be permanently scarred. Uncertainly, I tried to reassure her that we had not been in the fire long enough for that to happen.

Using a pocket torch, we checked how badly we were hurt. Kee's face, hands, wrists and feet had been burnt. I was slightly better off with a burn on my right upper arm and wrist. Kee found the ointment tube for burns, which we smeared on in thick layers. It provided some relief from the terrible pain. It was clear Kee would need medical help.

Despite our shock and fear, we had to continue. We hooked up the gas bottle to clean the rest of the filters. Hindered by our burns, it took a long time to put the final filter back in the housing and close the cab. Our situation was dire. We were drifting more than sailing, and the chance of running into severe weather had increased drastically this month. The cab had to be opened twice during Kee's watch for the perpetual filter treatment. Repeatedly blowing into an already redundant filter, fitting it, and then waiting for it to become idle again a few miles later seemed futile. But there was no alternative. I had to think. We were now adrift approximately 400 nautical miles west of Flores. We had no choice: we had to reach the island. Under ideal conditions, this would take only four days of relentless sailing if we worked night and day and had no technical problems. But we were injured, overtired, and had few reserves left.

I decided there was only one solution: pierce the paper filter to free the dirty oil path. The problem was that the delicate fuel pump would no longer have any protection and could be damaged beyond repair. When that happened, we would be in ultimate danger. It could take one day or a week before the engine fell silent forever – a considerable risk. I pierced the congested paper with a small screwdriver and fitted it again. It was our last chance.

> *Kee: I thought the explosion was the end of us. My face was in terrible pain, and I was convinced it would be permanently disfigured. Only later did I also feel the pain in other places, but my face remained the worst. Poor Fons was shaken; it was the first time I'd seen him like this. It was a good thing he'd been aware enough to turn off the gas immediately and throw milk across my face. He was in severe pain and was also terribly worried about me. Having treated our problems, we had to stop complaining and continue. After the miserable filter business, we nestled down against each other in the bunk from three to half past four. Then I woke up Fons because daylight appeared with fragments of light on the eastern horizon.*

At the first ray of sunshine, Kee checked out her burnt face in the mirror. Yellow pus oozed from the dark brown, scorched skin. Huge blisters had appeared on her fingers, hands and wrists, and her feet were raw.

A vague midday sun enabled me to measure our position, 350 miles due west of Flores. I dressed and bandaged Kee's face. We had to try to prevent the open wounds from getting infected. She could not do much with her hand. She was afraid her blackened face would remain disfigured. I tried to convince her everything would heal but that it would take time. To be honest, I wasn't entirely sure about that, but at least we were on our way to the civilised world where we could get help. The engine was running perfectly now the fuel could flow freely. However, I knew that the tiny dirt particles were eating up the precisely fitted fuel pump parts and that they would eventually destroy it.

At 7pm, we had a radio conversation with Amsterdam. To avoid alarming Kee's mother, I decided to say that I had some burn wounds and that Kee was alright. A nurse gave us instructions on how to treat the burns. We followed the advice to the letter, and Kee looked like an Egyptian mummy afterwards. For quite a while, she had had no appetite, which I found worrying since we needed lots of calories to keep our strength up.

A southern wind hurled large waves at our starboard side. Steering became one hell of a job again. Kee was dead on her feet, and I took over early. She had been gritting her teeth to make it. The compass light went out again because of the flooding seawater. Kee helped and shone the lamp while I used connectors and cables to fix the short circuit. It was getting impossible. Massive rainstorms and buckets of seawater thundered down onto the cab. The sea spray and flooding waves made it impossible to see the compass, so there was no question of keeping a course. The southerly wind reached severe gale force 9. Our sleeping bags lay in the water, which was running over the floor of the steering cab. It took another seven hours for the storm to subside and the wind to drop to a moderate breeze. During that time, all of Kee's head bandages became soaked and started coming apart.

> *Kee: As soon as it was light enough, I looked into the rearview mirror and scared myself to death. I had lost a piece of skin from my face. A bright pink spot was between the dirty, shrivelled, dark brown skin. There were brown stripes around my eyes, and yellow liquid oozed from my chin; how awful to arrive somewhere looking so ugly. My hands were at bursting point, and the pain was excruciating. My feet were in agony. I felt unhappy and deformed. But, on the positive side, I noticed my face hardly hurt anymore.*

The sky was bright and clear in the morning. We were relieved that Kee had not developed an infection. She felt deeply unhappy about her appearance. I kept comforting her, saying, 'Ahh, lass, it won't be for long,' not that it seemed to do much good. We were still 150 miles from the Azores and hoped for good navigation weather the following day. We could not afford to miss the island of Flores since the fuel pump would not last much longer, and we needed medical help. The stern tanks were mainly empty, so the propeller sometimes rose above the water, clawing wildly into the air. It made an ominous noise, but only lasted for a moment, so it did not harm the axles or the engine.

It was 10am when a mountain-like form emerged from between the masses of clouds. It was Flores, our only hope! Our midday longitude was 31° 41' W, only 26 miles from the island's west coast. To our surprise, we had covered 130 miles in the last 24 hours. We were finally blessed with good weather now we were nearing the island. Kee was frantically busy cleaning herself up. We decided to sail in a large arc towards the east.

*

Many ships have been crushed against the rocks because their captain ignored warnings, and we were almost one. We were only four miles from Santa Cruz das Flores. The engine had run at 1,200 rpm for almost four days without faltering, but I couldn't help wondering about the interior of the fuel pump, as nearly 500 litres of dirty diesel oil had flowed through it since piercing the filter.

As we sailed around a rock, we spotted the red flash of Santa Cruz's port directly in front of us. It was the middle of the night, so we had to wait for at least five hours before trying to enter the harbour. I didn't dare to stop the engine, so I dropped the rpm to 900, but disaster struck as the engine stalled! I feared there was no way we would get it going again. Was the fuel pump worn out?

The situation was dramatic – we lay in front of a dark, sleeping island with a dangerous, steep, rocky coast and fast unknown currents. Suffering a shipwreck so close to our target would be too much to bear. I tried to start the engine until the batteries were empty, but it was a nightmare. According to the pilot book, there was no marine telephone duty on the island, so we couldn't ask for help.

Slowly we drifted towards the menacing rocky coast. Thankfully, the weather was calm, but we had lost our sea anchor in a previous storm. We did what we could, tying together all the lines and heavy objects we could find to create a makeshift anchor. However, at 60 metres, there was still no grip to be had and the seabed, and the threat of being smashed against the rocks loomed. I warned Kee to prepare everything we needed to take with us in case we had to abandon ship and get into the rubber dinghy or life raft. Kee regularly shouted out to Flores, but there was no response.

To make matters worse, my back began freezing in agony when I jumped onto the deck during the disastrous engine activities. My hips were so twisted I could hardly stand. What should we do? The rocks were getting closer. As a last resort, I decided to use our small five horsepower rubber dinghy to pull the truck away from the coast.

The small outboard engine made such a racket that I couldn't hear Kee scream in pain when her burnt hands got caught in the taut line around the mast. Her enormous blisters and the raw flesh beneath were torn open. I abandoned my hauling attempts, feeling defeated. But then, as if the universe took pity on us, the currents changed – perhaps because the tide turned – and we slowly drifted away from the coast, towards the north-east, and into the open ocean! If only we were found in time before we drifted out of reach. Exhausted, we collapsed onto the deck. Kee fervently prayed for a happy ending.

The following day, we received the very welcome news that a Greek ship had heard us and had contacted the island of Corvo to report our situation. Kee kept trying to make contact, and eventually Radio Flores, likely operated by a fisherman, connected with us. An operator on Corvo, who spoke English, acted as an interpreter and helped establish communication.

We kept a lookout for a white boat that would come to tow us. After some time, we saw one sailing along the coast, looking out for us. We lay further out at sea, and the sun behind us blinded them. They disappeared momentarily but returned after receiving new landmarks over the radio. It was almost impossible to make them understand they were looking for a square shaped 'camião', not a yacht. After some back and forth, they finally saw us.

We were safe!

The men from the fast ten-metre-long motorboat greeted us in surprise. A father with his sons, they kept shouting through the marine telephone: 'Camião, camião!' One of the boys paddled towards us in a boat, climbed on board, attached the towing line and directed us to sit calmly on the deck while they arranged everything. I found it hard to relinquish control, but Kee ordered me to sit down and listen to them, since these experienced fishermen were probably the most skilled in these waters. And so we set off towards a safe haven, feeling both relieved and happy.

Victor, one of the fishermen, sailed swiftly between the rocks and reefs until the port appeared out of nowhere. He had told the whole population about the sailing 'camião' with its wounded crew, and they eagerly awaited our arrival, standing on the quay's low wall and the steps behind it. Local fishermen expertly guided us to the pier where willing hands immediately took the lines from us.

We were exhausted, ragged, wounded and sick, but all our tension had melted away, replaced by an overwhelming sense of gratitude and joy.

> *Kee: My relief at arriving was subdued considerably by my dreadful appearance. I had done as much as possible to look better, scrubbed myself down, smeared body lotion all over, cut my hair and then covered my face with cream so I was white as a sheet. It looked better than the dirty, stained condition I'd been in earlier. The cream did not*

stay on, unfortunately. I hoped that all my shrivelled skin would fall off so I could go into the new country with new skin. But what did it all matter anyway after that fateful night? We had been saved! The people on the quay stared at us as if we were wonders of the world. An islander pulled me onto the pier with such strength that I soared through the air like a featherlight elf and landed in the crowd. My exhaustion evaporated immediately, and I felt high on the experience of safety and friendly people around me. At the hospital, a French and a Portuguese doctor worked together. The Portuguese doctor was shocked by my appearance. She cut off all the blisters that had been torn open, treated the wounds with disinfectant and bandaged everything. My face began to tighten and burn terribly. In some places, the skin burst off. Fons's right upper arm was bandaged. I thought the way we were packaged up was somewhat excessive. They told us that Fons needed to lie down to rest his back and that I had to come back every day for my burns to be treated.

Our friend Hans arrived with a new fuel pump and six filters. What a relief! He also produced some photos of Robin, who seemed to be beaming with good health and had grown a lot. Kee immediately started showing the images proudly.

I replaced the worn fuel pump with the new one straight away. The injection time had to be calibrated very precisely, and then the engine started immediately. I placed a new filter on and cut off the tanks containing dirty oil. After a few days rest and recuperation, *Floating Truck* was ready to travel again. With the new fuel pump, she ran just like she used to. Kee and I were also slowly recovering from stress and exhaustion.

*

On 28 September, the weather cleared up and it was time to leave. We had been on Flores for 14 days. Hans sailed with us for the first part of the journey as we delivered him to the airport on the island of Faial, 130 miles to the south-east of Flores. We cast off and found our way between the dangerous rocks, although an increasing south-west wind roughed the sea up right away. A three-person crew made a huge difference in our watch-keeping. It was a pity it was just for one day. As always, after we'd been on land, Kee was seasick. We left her to rest as much as possible. Now that I could share the steering with Hans, that was no problem, although Hans later told us that he had found it incredibly tough with just two people.

We made it to Faial late in the afternoon the next day, and Hans had to disembark immediately to catch his flight. Fortunately, the flight was delayed as usual, so he made it into the aircraft just in time.

Kee and I wanted to depart as soon as possible, but Fate had different plans for us. Twelve hours after leaving Flores, a violent storm had broken out, which arrived with us a few hours later. No ship could leave port. Our lines broke, and we had to buy new hawsers. The storm lasted for six whole days!

When we finally set out on our journey to the European mainland, our greatest fear was the weather as this stormy period was anything but ideal. According to the pilot chart, we would no longer benefit from the eastern currents since they turned due south to join the Canary Current. That cost us half a knot of speed, which meant that we would cover 12 miles less per day. The wind would take a predominantly northern direction. All these factors were likely to complicate the journey.

Kee: I was dreading the last stage of the journey as I thought about what we would have to endure before being back home with Robin. But I did not have a moment's doubt that we should carry on and complete the voyage, because Fons had to face this technical and maritime challenge. If he was going to do it no matter what, I could not miss this adventure that pushed me beyond all my limits. So, I was ready to give all I had to complete it and taste that enormous victory over my fears. I didn't want to let him down. I preferred being in danger with him to sitting worried on land, waiting for him. Fons was worried too. We looked at each other, hugged one another, and thought the same thing: what are we up against? Would we have to try to save ourselves from awful circumstances again? Fons said: 'We will soon be in Portugal, just ten days to go!'

In two days, we covered 200 miles! It was a whole different experience now we were spared the terrible fuel problems. In Flores, I had rewired the compass lighting, this time using a much thicker cable and waterproof connectors. Kee was doing a lot better and kept singing arias. In the evening, we saw navigation lights moving towards the north-east. The shipping traffic was increasing now that we were getting closer to Europe.

We sailed east for four days without problems. Then, while removing the condensation water from the water separator, the engine's familiar hum suddenly stopped. We had to tilt the cab yet again. I soon discovered the cause: a clogged-up strainer. Just in case, I also replaced the filter near the engine. After ventilating it, the engine started without any issues. Under blue skies, working with the sextant was easy, and we soon knew we were 500 miles from Lisbon. We progressed calmly at 39° 12' N which was perfect since Lisbon is at 38° 40'.

As we got closer to Lisbon, we had to be extra careful. The chance of encountering ships here was much higher than on the open sea. But there was nothing to see. Soon, we were just 50 miles from the Portuguese coast. That meant we had only 12 hours left to sail. It all felt very tense and surreal. Our destination was close but we still couldn't see land in the evening. Darkness had already fallen when the four flashes of light from the Cabo da Roca lighthouse shone before us. All night, we kept the gear stick in neutral but waited for dawn in the driver's cab. We were looking for landmarks we could recognise. Hundreds of lights on the rocky coast called out to us like never before. In the east, the sky had a bright canopy of light and behind the mountain lay the metropolis of Lisbon. Robin and our friend Marion were there somewhere. It felt impossible to imagine.

As soon as it became light, we washed thoroughly and put on our best clothes. I had informed radio amateur Jan that we might arrive just before midday at the Monument of the Discoveries. He had passed on the message to Marion. We sailed onto the River Tagus. It was Saturday, and the crews of many pleasure boats waved at us. Some hours later, we sailed past the familiar seafaring monument celebrating Portugal's Age of Discovery with the statue of Henry the Navigator taking foremost place amongst explorers, monarchs and cartographers.

Suddenly, I saw Robin on the river bank. I told Kee, but she couldn't see clearly and had difficulty believing it. But I was right: Marion and little blond Robin in his buggy were there waving at us. It was a very emotional reunion.

There was nowhere we could moor, so after sailing for another quarter of an hour, we sailed into the fishing port of Doca de Santo Amaro. Marion ran along the quay with us, pushing Robin in his buggy. But the water was shallow, and we ran aground in the middle of the dock. It took a whole hour before the rising River Tagus brought in enough water for us to pull the rudder out of the sand. All that time, Marion and Robin were waiting on the quay, shouting and waving at us. Finally, we tied up and climbed onto the quay in a rush to be reunited with our son. It was the 52nd day after leaving the United States, the end of 1984, and we were going home to Amsterdam. I already had new travel plans, and Kee discovered she was pregnant. It was the perfect ending to our challenging and eventful truck drive across the Atlantic.

End of a voyage, docked in Lisbon

Racing the Waves
Flying Bottle

The *Bottle* project was born on our *Last Generation* rafting voyage when we threw a message in a bottle into the ocean. Watching the wind and the currents carry it away, I resolved to one day build a vessel in that shape.

In 1985, we were living in Amsterdam. In that bustling, cosmopolitan capital, I had the idea of winning the Blue Riband, a prestigious accolade awarded to the fastest Atlantic crossing between the United States and Europe. Since July 1952, the record had been held by the *United States*, an American passenger ship that had covered the 2,906 nautical mile route from the Ambrose Lightship off New York to Bishop Rock off the Scilly Isles in three days, 12 hours and 12 minutes. I wanted to do it in three days, which would require an average speed of 40 knots, nearly 75 kilometres per hour. Back then, nobody had tried to beat the record and only very few knew of its existence. The voyage had to be completed without stopping or refuelling – an imposing feat for any small ship.

Five years after throwing that first bottle into the ocean, my bizarre dream began to take shape. I wanted to design, construct and test a vessel that was a bottle-shaped hydrofoil to make an attempt on the Blue Riband.

There was interest from an engineering company, but their technicians thought it almost impossible to single-handedly tackle all the different disciplines that would arise during the construction. This was a mix of marine and aeronautics. But for me that was precisely what made the technical challenge so exciting. Shipbuilding, hydraulics, pneumatics, engines, electronics and aircraft construction were already familiar to me. The challenge was to bring them all together into one vessel – *Flying Bottle*.

First, *Flying Bottle* would have to be placed on high legs with wings, or foils, to cut through the ocean waves at speed. The average swell on the planned crossing was three metres. This required robust materials. Kee took on the job of finding those materials and securing sponsorship. From a shipyard, I collected four books and eleven reports about the problems related to hydrofoil systems. For weeks I studied the mechanics of aircraft construction and hydrofoil vessels. To visualise the complex machine, I built a small wooden model. Next, it was time to build a larger, four-metre-scale bottle as a prototype.

Curious eyes on Fons with model bottle

Once the tests on this proved encouraging, it was time to build the full-size vessel itself.

Finding a suitable tank for the full-scale *Flying Bottle* was a challenge, but Kee was successful. A company that made boilers offered to give us a seven-metre-long, cylindrical tank with a diameter of just over two metres at no cost. I took a truck to collect it, then put it on wheels, so it was easier to manoeuvre. So both the one-third scale prototype and the full-size *Flying Bottle* continued to be built together. After several months, the prototype bottle looked great with its

Scale model Flying Bottle *prototype*

crown cap. We made a crane in the docks and lowered the little 'beer' bottle into the water. I would now determine if the engine and the propeller for the prototype were the right choices by trial and error. It was the beginning of a long period of different experiments.

For the full-size *Flying Bottle,* a dealer selling American marine diesel engines provided a Detroit 1,000 horsepower engine, as used in US coastguard boats. The beautiful machine weighed 1,400 kilograms. The promised sponsorship for this never turned up. Eventually, I had to pay for the engine myself.

The propeller for the large *Flying Bottle* finally arrived from Cologne. It was a beautiful five-bladed, 60-centimetre propeller designed for high speed. Kee and I were allowed to visit the factory, where they used to make special propellers for submarines, and we were impressed. There were even giant propellers with a diameter of ten metres. To fit our propeller, I had to hack a big hole in the concrete floor. Tackling many different things concurrently led to a chaotic work schedule. Many people found it challenging to work with me, but I found clarity amid the chaos.

Our plans gained public interest when they were featured in *The Saturday Paper*. The full-page article caught the attention of Freddy Heineken, the brilliant boss of the Heineken Breweries, who offered sponsorship. This was exciting news, but I was disappointed when the brewery's PR department, rather than their technical team, was put in charge of our project. Heineken immediately set out to give both *Flying Bottle* and the prototype bottle a makeover, turning them into their iconic green export beer bottles. From that point on, Kee had regular, time-consuming meetings and evaluations in Amsterdam at the Heineken headquarters.

The PR department hired a professor from the Delft University of Technology to act as their advisor. This led to long delays. The academic did not understand the project at all and started by asking which was the hydrofoil's front and back. He knew nothing about hydrofoil systems. His expertise, it turned out, was in constructing harbours. He continually answered my questions with a vague: 'Could be.'

Despite the delays and many technical problems, the construction finally reached the point where we could make a test trip with the large *Flying Bottle*. It was too big to leave the workshop – so the building had to be broken down carefully around it. With a lot of noise, dust and flying debris, a demolition team disassembled our workshop within a few days. We lowered the vessel into the water for the first time using the demolition crane. It was an emotional moment, and it proved the *Bottle*'s perfect positioning in the water. Kee had to wipe away a few tears.

> **Kee:** *This was a time of momentous celebrations and my emotions were always close to the surface. Fons and I were married in Amsterdam exactly ten years after we started living together. The event was attended by our families and friends and even the PR people from Heineken. Only my brother Vincent from Brazil was absent, as he celebrated his birthday that day. Neither Fons nor I wanted to wear a ring, so we hung necklaces around each other's necks with the symbols for faith, hope and love. These symbols connected our past experiences to our hopes for the future, which was to include* Flying Bottle's *maiden voyage.*

Following the professor's advice, we moved the Heineken *Bottle* to a shipyard for the final stage of completion. He told us that would be faster and more professional. Naturally, it worked out differently in practice. The PR department wanted to plan all sorts of things but did not realise the vessel was still at an experimental stage. By this point, I'd had enough. The person at the company I connected with, Freddy Heineken, had sadly stepped down as chairman and CEO after his high-profile kidnapping. The people we were now working with didn't have his visionary sprit and drive. I felt out of place and decided I couldn't keep working like this. So I wrote a clear letter to the new Heineken director, saying I could no longer work according to their PR department's policies. Being attached to Heineken made no sense if it meant I could not develop my technical ideas – especially the improved propulsion. So, over a year after we reached our agreement with Heineken, our cooperation came to an end. We were given a cheque to pay for open invoices, such as the engine, and I felt liberated and relieved.

We pulled off the Heineken labels and re-painted our *Flying Bottle* and the prototype white. We made a new start, but we realised that since the brewery had used *Flying Bottle* in their publicity, it would be difficult to find another sponsor.

At home, I went back to the drawing board to design a new propulsion system and continued to make regular test trips with the prototype bottle. By that time, we had fine-tuned her so well that she performed splendidly, requiring only 20 metres before take-off and reaching a speed of 33 knots. Furthermore, the prototype vessel had excellent manoeuvrability and was very stable.

The automatic height control worked perfectly when we tested it on the full-scale *Flying Bottle,* Racing across the ocean at a speed of 40 knots meant we needed excellent visibility in front of us. At an airport in the south of the Netherlands, our friend

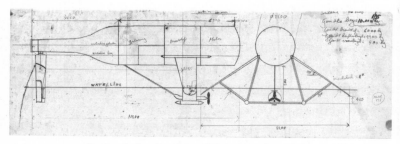

Section design drawings of Flying Bottle *and foils*

Peter found two Republic F-84 Thunderstreak fighter planes with cockpits intact – including the ejection seats, although we had no use for those. They were destined for the dump, so we were able to take them. The transparent, durable, double-walled canopies that could resist enormous wind speeds were perfect for our needs. After a lot of tinkering we connected one of the cockpits to *Flying Bottle*. It looked sturdy, and the visibility outside was perfect. I worked on the cockpit's electrical system for a week to make it foot-operated since the pilot would otherwise be short of hands to operate all the foils and rudders.

Flying Bottle had a hydraulically driven rudder, elevator control rod, ailerons, propeller, anchor winch and chairs. Rob Fintelman from Findynamica gave us the many components necessary to install the extensive hydraulic system. We worked for months with varying degrees of success. We had now arrived at the point where we could do test runs at full speed. To do these as safely as possible, I filled the large 12,100-litre tanks with just 500 litres of fuel for our three-kilometre test runs.

The Detroit diesel engine and the new propulsion worked perfectly. The challenge with *Flying Bottle* was to take the drive forward from the engine and through two angled turns down to the propeller, which was two and a half metres below the engine level, beneath the hydrofoil wings. We used two MAN truck differentials from one of their biggest trucks to take the drive through the first 120° turn and then down at an angle of 45°, before making another 45° turn to the propeller. The differentials reduced the initial 3,500 rpm at the first stage of the drive shaft to the required 750 rpm at the prop. There were no vibrations, and the automatic stabilisation worked surprisingly well.

Kee, sitting in the co-pilot's seat, found our full-speed test run marvellous, despite getting soaked by the water that streamed in through the open hatch.

There was still a lot to be done regarding the organisational side of the project, but I considered the technical aspect complete. The development and construction of *Flying Bottle* was an enormous challenge that required extreme efforts from both Kee and me. Fortunately, the good moments outnumbered the bad, and we were helped by fantastic people who selflessly made their energy, knowledge and materials available to us.

Then, we learnt Richard Branson was making plans to break the speed record, albeit refuelling during the crossing. With his name and resources behind his endeavour I felt my efforts to cross without fuelling were going to be diminished.

After a long period of designing, building and testing, I also recognised that I had been working on the project for too long and had lost my enthusiasm. So, when the construction

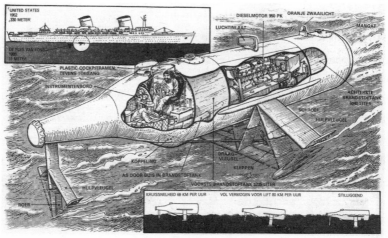

Press illustration of Flying Bottle *with her Blue Riband hopes*

site where we had designed and worked on so many of our inventions was sold, we decided to round off that beautiful and happy period of our lives. Our sons, Robin and Brendan, had grown up there and had enjoyed a fun and adventurous youth. Now it was time to move on.

I dismantled the legs, foils and drive system from the full-size *Flying Bottle* and destroyed the hydrofoil components. I had completed the critical elements of the *Flying Bottle* project successfully testing both the prototype and the full-size *Flying Bottle*. I never attempted to win the Blue Riband. In hindsight, just knowing I had successfully created a vessel capable of winning without a refuelling stop was enough for me.

The *Bottle* was no longer a high-speed hydrofoil, and I had thoughts of converting her into a sailing craft at some point in the future, and then crossing the Atlantic in her. Having removed the legs and hydrofoils, I had to design and make stability fins and a rudder and install another far more modest propulsion system. The *Bottle*'s large machinery room and fuel tanks would have to be changed into a small engine room, kitchen and toilet. I would need to cut a piece from the hull to create a steering house, requiring the removal of all kinds of excessive parts and engine mounts with a blow torch. After that, new partitions would have to be welded with sheet steel to make room for future propulsion systems. There were many months of work ahead, and I wasn't ready for it yet.

I held on to the working *Flying Bottle* prototype and moved the now legless full-size *Flying Bottle* into storage at my brother's metal company in northern Belgium.

From Speed to Sail

Message in a Bottle

It wasn't until the summer of 1997 – when, after 15 years in Amsterdam, Kee and I decided to move to Antwerp – that we resumed work on the *Bottle*. We found the perfect workshop space in one of the many old empty buildings in the north of Antwerp, which would eventually be demolished. After contacting the port services, we managed to get an excellent location for low rent. Once the municipality installed electricity and water, work could begin.

Michielsen's Cranes was our sponsor for hoisting and transport work, and they brought the *Bottle* to the new work haven using a 35-tonne crane and a matching trailer. A lot of pushing and shoving was necessary to press the vessel through the door and get her inside. It took our small crew three years before a beautiful, rebuilt *Bottle* could be driven back outside. And it wasn't until 2004 that the *Bottle* was ready to sail across the Atlantic.

The workshop had slowly been filled with welding machines, oxygen and gas bottles, materials and tools. I started work with renewed enthusiasm. Kee came by on her bicycle every afternoon, so we could eat together and talk about business. She was busy making new contacts and tracking down suitable suppliers.

A 50-centimetre-long model of the *Bottle* that I pulled through the water showed that the hull speed was around five knots and that a marine engine of 80 horsepower would be enough. We chose an 85-horsepower five-cylinder Nanni. Six weeks later, a truck drove a heavy crate containing the new diesel engine into the workshop. Now I could begin to weld the engine mounts and place connectors for fuel and engine controls.

For months I worked on the technical aspects of the project alone. I often worked with blowtorches, sparking grinding machines, high-pressure systems and a powerful current of 400 volts. Although I regularly had minor injuries from flying metal fragments and melting steel or severe blows against steel protrusions, I was fortunate to be spared any serious injuries.

Daniel, a friend of mine, decided to take leave so he could come and help me daily. He would be coming along on the *Bottle*

Welding work on the Flying Bottle *nose*

as a crew member. A while later, his friend Stijn also joined the team to assist with the electrical installations.

Discovering that the *Bottle* would be mooring in Dakar, Daniel and Stijn decided to travel to Senegal on their motorbikes and join the *Bottle* there. Meanwhile, Daniel's long-standing relationship had broken down and he took it badly for a while. Then, some weeks later he introduced us to Nina, his new girlfriend! This resulted in Nina planning to join Daniel for the long journey to Dakar, riding on the back of his motorcycle. Stijn's unattached and now upset girlfriend would stay behind in Belgium. We regularly drank a beer to all these developments in our little office.

*

However, something unexpected and unpleasant was about to place the entire project in jeopardy. I was used to working long days and had no problems lugging heavy materials around. Kee and I made long bicycle trips, and I did not get tired. But since we would once again be going for a long voyage alone, without medical help, I'd had a wide range of medical tests done, and up to that point, the results had all been good. To round off the sequence, I visited a cardiologist, even though I was convinced that, without symptoms, I had no heart problems. But to my surprise, the classical bicycle test showed something was not right. A further examination of my capillary system showed that my coronary artery was 70% blocked and I needed a bypass operation as soon as possible. It was a complicated operation requiring a long period of recovery.

On the day of the operation, Kee and I cycled to the hospital. In their large garden, I saw a sign for the morgue. I was afraid and hoped I would not end up there. That evening nurses shaved me as smooth as a baby, and I had to wash with a special disinfecting soap. I felt emotional and had to say goodbye to my dear Kee, maybe forever. In the operating theatre masked men and women dressed in green waited for me. One man stepped towards me, and then everything went dark.

It seemed only a few seconds before a dim light fell across my eyes. Ten hours had passed. Through a jungle of tubes, pipes and bags of liquid, I saw Kee, Robin and Brendan again. My whole body hurt, and I was breathing fast and with difficulty. They had put four bypasses in place, using veins from my legs. The operation was a success.

I was back home in a week with prescribed homework of rest and physiotherapy. But I had no time for such things, and after another week struggled to the workshop to rejoin my friends Daniel and Stijn, who had continued everything related to the *Bottle* while I had been away. The question was whether I could ignore my doctors' advice unpunished. It was unwise, but I had no choice as far as I was concerned. Fortunately, I recovered fast and was even able to manage without medicine.

I welded a streamlined half-metre-deep, five-metre-long keel under the *Bottle*. In Rotterdam, we picked up 800 kilograms of lead ballast which we packed in the keel. As a final preparation, we gave the *Bottle* her third livery. After her previous flying colours of green, and later white, the converted *Message in a Bottle* was now painted royal blue.

It was time to go.

As expected, rolling the *Bottle* out of the workshop was not easy. We put temporary wheels on the sides and used pulleys to get her outside, where a crane lifted all eight tonnes of her onto the trailer and then onto the nearby quay to await launch.

The next day, after a restless night, we drove to the quays early. Kee had organised a festive event once again. I had to keep calm. My thorax, which had been sawn open and tied back together using steel wire, still prevented me from making specific movements. Kee thought it inappropriate for the *Bottle*'s christening to involve smashing a fellow bottle. In a thrift shop, she had found a glass mermaid and filled this with an alcoholic drink. Kee threw the mermaid towards the hull with the words: 'We christen you *Message in a Bottle* and wish you a successful mission. May you be protected on your journey and have a safe return!' The mermaid smashed into thousands of shiny pieces. The crane's heavy cables became taut, and *Message in a Bottle* swung above the dock water. The tension was released from the wires precisely at the waterline, and the vessel was floating. We were so relieved! The next day we pulled *Message in a Bottle* another 100 metres along the quay.

I placed a straight tube on the keel to construct a base for the masts. It rose two metres above the deck. Using a specially designed frame, we hoisted the poles upwards and let them descend into the hull. The next step was to test the engine with the hydraulic drive system I had devised and installed to turn the new propeller. It did a great job, and its fuel consumption turned out to be just five litres an hour at a speed of five knots.

*

Kee contacted a shipping agent and found a shipping line. *Message in a Bottle* would depart on a general cargo ship named *Marcel*, sailing to Tenerife in the Canary Islands.

Film and video specialist Wim Robberechts, our regular advisor and supplier of materials for more than 30 years, delivered a complete set of film equipment in watertight cases that we could borrow.

It was time to sail *Message in a Bottle* to the loading bay for our first real sailing trip. Thick mist lay across the docks, making it difficult to find our destination, but the green ship we were looking out for was not far away. The Antwerp dock workers – the best and fastest in the world – had no trouble getting our ship on board *Marcel*, and they skilfully and carefully secured her.

Kee and I flew ahead to Tenerife, and in the port of Santa Cruz we saw the green-hulled ship carrying our blue bottle slowly coming into view. It was a touching moment. Our vessel remained on the quay for two days, and we lived in her. After *Marcel* had departed, the dockhands lowered *Message in a Bottle* into the water. The life raft was attached to the deck with a quick-release clasp, and the Epirb-satellite distress beacon was bolted in the cockpit.

Kee searched through Santa Cruz to collect the necessary materials and food, guided by the lack of a cooling system onboard. Our fuel tanks were full, but we wanted to carry extra fuel with us. It was about 900 miles to Cabo Verde. If the wind did not cooperate – and it did not look as if it would as it remained southern and was, therefore, a headwind for us - we would have to use the engine to cover most of this leg. Finally, we hoisted the two masts and attached the sails.

*

21 March 2006: photographers and filmmakers took their last few shots while friends and the harbour police wished us a safe journey. The hawsers were pulled from the bollards and thrown on board. I turned *Message in a Bottle* towards the harbour exit and took the engine up to 1,400 rpm. The adventure was about to begin. As with our earlier vessels we had not had the chance to put *Message in a Bottle* through sea trials. Many had voiced doubts about our strange vessel's sailing capabilities with a cork in the front instead of a sharp bow. This was the hour of truth.

An unstable, mostly southerly wind still blew across the Canary Islands, making it impossible for us to sail, so we depended on the engine. *Message in a Bottle* rocked, but less than we had expected. We followed the east coast of Tenerife, standing together in the cockpit, feeling very alert and experiencing every moment with trepidation. As sunset neared, we were level with the island's southern coast. We left jagged rocks behind us in a golden glow. Navigational beacons lit up in the distance. We went into the night, gave each other a firm hug and exchanged wishes for all to go well.

Now we had left the island's shelter, the sea changed. High waves attacked us from all sides and made *Message in a Bottle* rock terribly. Our ship did not appear in danger of capsizing, and we were never seasick, but we had to cling on, and we received our fair share of bumps and bruises. Tiredness soon struck us. For weeks, we had been busy day and night, and now our bodies had to adjust to extreme ocean conditions again. The weather soon became colder, so we donned our warm survival suits that made us feel safe. Our feet remained stone-cold because of the continuous flow of water coming into the cockpit through the scuppers. I regularly checked the engine instruments and felt the engine and the hydraulic drive that turned the prop to make sure they did not get too hot. The releaser and the constant velocity joint did get warm, which worried me a little. I reduced our rpm to 1,200.

The automatic pilot worked perfectly. Steering without it would have been an almost impossible task. At times, a massive wave would come at us sideways, threatening to throw us off course, so the hydraulics on the automatic steering had their work cut out and squeaked and groaned terribly. But we rarely heard the off-course signal, which we had set at 20 degrees.

There was a waning moon, which appeared rather late. The wind was still variable, and as a result, so was the wave pattern. Our watch-keeping was disorderly that first night. We could not even settle down peacefully in the small wheelhouse since we kept having to cling to something to save us from sliding around.

We were happy when dawn broke. The south wind was picking up. *Message in a Bottle* turned out to be seaworthy and always fought her way back to the top when huge waves washed over us. The neck with the cork sometimes dived deep into the water, but it always straightened itself up quickly. It turned out that we had covered 100 miles in the last 24 hours. Our Nanni engine enabled our ship to do four knots. All things being equal, we would need the weather to play ball and provide fair weather to reach the Cabo Verde island of São Vicente; if that worked out, we would then require 1,100 litres of fuel for the trip. As that was the exact amount we carried, it was risky. We knew from experience that losing control approaching the island would mean we would smash against the rocks.

Kee: Fons was busy checking and tidying everything, so I went to write. It was quite a task. My pen went in all

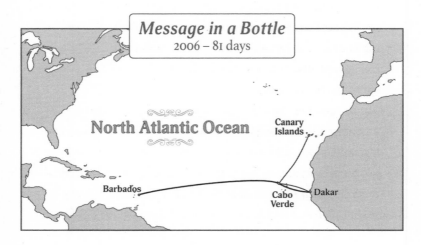

directions. Inside, we had to perform acrobatics just to move around. Everything that had been secured was now dislodged. There was no single moment without excessive movement. We used muscles in our body we never knew we had.

There was no cardan stove on board since the man who built our galley had no idea how to make something like that. I had to wedge between the worktop and the toilet door to hold on to the kettle to boil some water. I could not stay inside for long without getting seasick. The most comfortable place was lying in the bunk wedged between the wall and the plank we put up to prevent us from falling out during rough seas.

At sunset, a whole school of dolphins appeared to say hello. They played around and jumped on both sides of the bottleneck. I did not dare step onto the deck to go out to the front. I could easily be flung off and fall into the ocean. We only had a low, thin, flexible railing at the stern, with no protection forwards. There, we had to cling to the mast. Fons lay wrapped up on the couch in the wheelhouse. He had found a way to clamp himself in place.

When I woke up later, Fons was anxiously checking the hydraulic drive with his torch. It was making a strange sound and was the only large unit for which he had no spare parts. All kinds of horror scenarios passed in front of my eyes. He changed the rpm so that the engine made less noise, and thankfully Message in a Bottle *behaved less violently. We had to watch the quantity of diesel in the jerrycan carefully as another had to be connected before it was empty. No air could come into the engine's fuel pipes because it would stall; if that happened, ventilating it would be quite a job. We had not forgotten the fuel problems during our crossing with our* Floating Truck.

A strong southern wind blew the next day. With breaking waves raging at us from the side, neither of us felt well, and it was all we could do to stay upright. If we continued like this, we were afraid we would not have enough fuel to reach our goal, the port of Mindelo on São Vicente. Feeling brave, we tipped the two canisters containing doubtful diesel into the large tank. I filled an empty five-litre bottle with diesel oil so we could connect it to the engine and see how long it would take for the fuel to be used up. The result was just over four litres per hour at 1,200 rpm – precisely what I had calculated.

Message in a Bottle continued to dive and rock in the chaotic seas. We had several incidents when the engine stalled after I fell against the ignition key. The first time I did this Kee was terrified the engine had died.

There were now high, irregular waves coming at us diagonally across our stern. We had to try to hoist our small junk sail, but doing any manoeuvre on deck was dangerous. We unrolled the sail that was secured on the deck. Our swaying and the fact we had no grip meant we could easily be pushed out under the railing and fall into the sea.

Kee pulled at the halyards from the wheelhouse, but the sheet remained stuck behind the sail. After releasing the rope, I swayed about dangerously, finding that it was impossible to get the sail in a position that would improve our course, or our speed. We lowered the whole thing again and had to roll up and tie down the canvas. Would a mainsail be better for us, or was it simply not possible to sail *Message in a Bottle*?

The weather calmed eventually. Before long, the sun was beaming down, the ocean was deep blue and the dolphins came every day. That might sound heavenly, but in reality, I was constantly worried about the hydraulic drive because a mechanical problem always seemed an imminent threat. The failure of a tiny part would be enough to bring us into danger. I never truly relaxed.

Nevertheless, we had reached halfway on the first leg of our route, covering 418 miles. Our blue bottle had passed with flying colours. The chart showed us we were on the same route as our voyage in *Seaview*. I did not dare to believe we only had four days to go and would make it with the available fuel. We had a large swell that night, and the waves hit us beam on. The movement was horrendous, but we tried to focus on the stars, which were amazing. A beautiful, slim bird with a long pintail flew above us for a while. It wanted to land to rest but did not dare because of our rolling around. The navigation lights no longer worked. I replaced the fuse, but it did not

With the wind from behind, it made sense to try out the sails

help, so I stopped the engine to examine the electrical wiring in the engine room. *Message in a Bottle* immediately swung round, bringing the wind onto our starboard. Now that the wind came a little more from behind, it made sense to try out the sails to see if that would give us more stability. But at that point, we could not muster the courage or the strength. In the meantime, Daniel, his girlfriend Nina and Stijn were on their way to Senegal on their motorcycles.

We often thought about Robin, Brendan, our family and friends. A lot of people were worrying about us, and we had no way of making contact. The aerial had to be secured on the deck with great care, requiring acrobatics we were not prepared to risk. The sun was scorching. We threw the remaining diesel oil from the canisters together in one container. What was supposed to be a simple task became a hellish trial that left us greasy and stinking.

> *Kee: For the first time, I felt up to the challenge of cooking. First, I had to carve a path for myself between the escaped objects that had fallen onto the floor so I could collect a can of meatballs and another containing peas and white beans from the floor. They all went into a pan with a finishing touch of eight pressed cloves of garlic. After a lot of cursing and bruising, I took a bowl of hot food to Fons in the wheelhouse, giving us the kick we both needed. Fons ate very well. I ate less, but the taste was still delicious. In the evening, Fons also had some chocolate and crackers.*
>
> *That night, we did not feel tired, and we sat in the wheelhouse with our headlights on, reading while* Message in a Bottle *was dancing, diving and rolling. We both held on to the lifting hook at the back of the wheelhouse with one hand.*

We squeezed ourselves into our survival suits as soon as the sun went under, which made peeing in the narrow heads a drama as far as I was concerned. While I clung to the brace on one side of the wall, I had to push down the whole suit with my other hand. The tension, the worry and the inconvenience of it all did not subside. I never got used to it.

There were sprays of foam all around us, waves from behind, which mostly dived under us and passed through. They also came at us beam on — indicating a good northeasterly trade wind at last. A sea turtle swam past us, and sea swallows dived around us. The dolphins continued to visit us at sunrise and sunset, but the mountainous high sea remained. Despite adjusting the course the previous day, we had drifted towards the east.

Message in a Bottle toiled away endlessly. For days, the cork had been pounding into the water with huge splashing blows. At least it was coping well. Every three hours, I entered our position on the map. We had to be able to adjust our course as quickly as possible. If anything were to go wrong, it might take months before we landed, starving in the Caribbean.

The salty, aggressive seawater made our electrical connections put on a full display of malfunctions. The navigation lights, the top light, the bow propeller and the anchor winch were not working. I had to rewire a lot of things and twist myself under the dashboard and into the heat of the engine room to do so.

The pot of Nescafé fell out of the cupboard, and the floor was full of sticky, brown goo. The same thing happened to the container with milk powder. Everything had come loose and was lying on the ground – a big heap of chaos. We picked ourselves up and found the energy to secure everything again.

Atlantic Archipelago
Message in a Bottle

At last we were heading in the right direction and making good progress. At 6am, I saw lights in the distance. It had to be Santo Antão, the most western island of the Cabo Verde archipelago. As it became lighter, we also saw our destination of São Vicente in the distance. We hoped Marc, our friend on the island, had arranged a berth so that we could moor on the quayside.

We had an even harder time when we came close to the islands. High, angry waves and deep valleys meant the Canal de São Vicente, the strait between the two islands, was suddenly much shallower. *Message in a Bottle* jumped, reared up, dived and ploughed, struggling her way forwards like a wild mustang. Every time the cork dived into the waves the water washed over us like an exploding fountain. We saw the tops of an impressive rocky outcrop glowing red in the rising sun.

Then we saw the sharp rocks in front of the entrance to the port of Mindelo. The ferry boat from Santo Antão came sailing past. Sailing into harbour, with the rocks to port, we were amazed how much had changed since we last entered it with *Seaview* several years before. Then, there had been just one quay and maybe a fishing boat and a little fish factory. Now, Japanese companies had added an industrial port, a fishing port, and a pier for luxury yachts. So many houses had been constructed around it. It looked like Mindelo had become a large town. We saw a lot of cars driving around where there used to be just a couple. We discovered that our first mooring on the quay was only for large ships, so we continued to the pier. A man in a boat came alongside and explained that Marc had reserved a space for us there. However, we had to anchor while we waited because another repair job was underway. That was a problem since our anchor winch did not work. Two locals came to our assistance in a small boat. We attached our anchor to long lines they threw out from their ship, but the lines did not stay in place because the bottom was solid rock. The men had an idea and signalled for us to follow them. They motored to a decaying, rusty ship against which we could moor. We chose not to. Instead, we went back to drop anchor again. I had to pull in the port anchor three times, but then it worked.

> *Kee: One hour later, Marc's son Sven came roaring up in a little boat. Marc was away overseas, and Sven had secured a temporary spot for us in a small old shipyard at the other side of the bay. So we hoisted the anchors again and sailed in the opposite direction. In the shipyard's small harbour were a few old boats and a luxury French fishing boat. Using a rope as thick as a wrist, we had to pull the ship towards the quay wall so we could jump across some stones and climb up the wall. I had to practice a few times before I could do it without fear.*
>
> *We received a lot of interest right away. In the wheelhouse of the ship were a crowd of boys and men. We later found out it was the regular place for curious onlookers to hang out. They could look diagonally into our*

cabin. Privacy was hardly possible. Much was stolen from us while we were sleeping: our two binoculars, camera, watch, flippers, snorkels, diving goggles and towels. We were lying in a typical poor neighbourhood and heard this was the preferred spot for thieving. We were advised to leave a guard on board whenever we left. Great! We just wanted rest and some food. I lost no time giving away the large bag with playthings for the children. Fons and I were so tired that we only managed to throw some stuff off the bunk and throw ourselves into it before we fell into a coma.

The next morning we had to go to the harbour master. I was in a rush but Kee reminded me that we had to adjust to the local rhythm of "Muito Tranquillo". We were not feeling well. Our legs behaved strangely, and our muscles were aching all over. Eventually we walked down unpaved paths alongside charming, poky houses, piles of rubbish and iron dumped by the side of the road.

We could no longer expect an official to pop by in person and accept a stamped Canarian invoice for diesel fuel as our shipping documentation, as had been the previous case on *Seaview*. We paid a small, fixed amount for our stay, however long that would be. We did not possess a visa, but that was no problem, probably because we were mariners. Customs officials stamped our passports.

We soon moved *Message in a Bottle* to the guarded pier Marc had arranged for us. It was safe there, but Kee had preferred our previous place with all the visits from young people. Nevertheless, it was still a friendly place. One evening, we were standing with Marc in a tiny dark shop drinking grogue – strong stuff, the national beverage, a sort of white rum – with El Géneral, a cheery retired sailor and close friend of Marc, who drank a litre of the stuff every day, spread throughout the day. Friends regularly came to play music. It could turn into a party at any time.

> *Kee: We continued to meet an extraordinary variety of people. One day, as I came through the gate, a tall, handsome black man approached me: 'Ola, where are you going? Give me your hand. I love you with all of my soul. I want a woman like you.'*
>
> *'Would you not rather have a younger woman?' I asked.*
>
> *'No, I want you. Do you have a man?' he said.*
>
> *'Yes,' was my obvious reply.*
>
> *'Oh! I want a white woman. My heart is breaking for you. Look, I have some nice necklaces.'*
>
> *'Yes, very nice. But I don't want anything.'*
>
> *'Okay, then. Look at me, give me your hand. Bye!'*
>
> *Another man was waiting for me: 'Ola Margarita, lovely woman, I love you, come sit with us again, kiss kiss. How are you?'*
>
> *By now, I had to fist bump with the others, as that was how they greeted each other here, and a few children were hanging around my knees. We talked for a while about men and women and how it is not pleasant to sleep alone. He told me that he was looking after a boat and had his wife or another woman come to sleep with him every night. He smelled strongly of grogue. A stranger came towards me, smiling as though we were old friends, shook my hand, asked how I was doing, my name, where I came from and if I had anything to eat.*

Back on board, I spent a lot of time in thinking how to improve *Message in a Bottle* to make sailing easier, because the route across to Senegal would be particularly tricky. There were few social amenities here – the focus was on survival, although those with money from abroad fared better. A mere 650 years ago, these islands had been uninhabited. The Portuguese discovered them and brought slaves captured on Ile de Gorée (close to Dakar) and Conakry Guinee. The archipelago had since filled with a mix of cultures as seafarers from all corners of the world discovered one of the world's most natural harbours in the old crater of a volcano.

Many paths and roads were still unpaved, and houses made from homemade rough stones were interspersed with flats in all sorts of colours in a criss-cross fashion. Walking through the streets, Kee never lacked attention. There were plenty of colourful and unpredictable encounters and invitations. The locals were direct and unfiltered and there was always something happening around us.

We spent two lovely days with Wim, the photographer and Jan, the journalist, making a documentary about Cabo Verde. We sailed offshore so that they could take some photographs of *Message in a Bottle* and trekked across São Vicente's lunar and Martian landscapes, through small oases, to capture the sea crashing against the rocks on the north coast. A meal in a deserted mountain house introduced us to the unique delicacy of sea slugs.

A visit to the neighbouring island of Santo Antão, revealed the untouched beauty of the archipelago in its green and fertile volcano crater, as clouds floating through the jagged peaks and donkeys transported everything from wood to water. There were goats and sometimes cows next to a house.

As we prepared ourselves, mentally and physically, for the challenging leg to Senegal, people warned us that it would be a heavy passage. This weighed on my mind. Kee took care of our provisions – mostly fresh vegetables and expensive canned food imported from Europe – but I was still apprehensive about the coming journey.

*

22 April, we departed from Mindelo to Dakar. After my maintenance work and running repairs, most of the teething troubles had been resolved. Everything seemed to be working well. We would do a detour, sailing alongside the south coast in the shelter of the archipelago because it was calmer than the rocky north coast. It would be a tough stretch for us with adverse currents and winds, and we were glad it was not too far, just short of 600 miles. The wind was blowing strongly, as always, and we were nervous.

As soon as we had passed São Vicente, the sea went wild again and we rolled and reared until we sailed into the shelter of the uninhabited islands of Santa Luzia and Branco. A few sharks came past, and a group of dolphins amused us. Dusk was already falling, and by the time we passed the rocky and precipitous island of Brava, it was dark. Suddenly, the alarm for the water cooling began to beep shrilly. I immediately turned off the engine and dived into the engine room, but everything looked fine. When we investigated further, we discovered the alarm was malfunctioning. Probably because some seawater had splashed its way past the dashboard and into the alarm system.

We had to pass the jagged rocky coastline of the island of São Nicolau in pitch-black darkness. Now it was the turn of the oil pressure alarm to shriek. More panic, turning the engine off again, diving into the engine room. But there was plenty of oil. That alarm was also affected by seawater. Our vessel rolled and dived, and we went along with it.

During the general inspection, we discovered a problem with the neck of *Message in a Bottle*. The stopper had disappeared from the pipe through which the anchor chain rolled. Water flowed in the neck and streamed through *Message in a Bottle*'s bilges to where the propeller shaft turned. The propeller shaft was the constant-velocity joint with the thrust-bearing, which should not rotate in seawater. We had to remove the floor piece above the propulsion to pump out the water using the bilge pump I'd placed there earlier as a precaution. The hatch above the shaft was incredibly hard to remove, and it cost us so much effort that we just left it open. However, that was dangerous as we had to be very careful not to step on the running axle every time we climbed in and out of the cabin, and we had to keep an eye on any water that might go in and pump it out immediately.

Things almost went badly wrong when we didn't see the steep, jagged rocky coast of São Nicolau in the ink-black darkness. Unaware of the situation, we drifted north because of the strong current and sailed directly towards a lethal rock

Under engine off the jagged coastline

wall. Thanks to the surf's sound, I was alerted to a jagged rock face outlined against the steep background just in time. I immediately changed course to due south and took the engine to its limit. Fearfully, we listened to the roaring sound of the breaking waves, hoping it would diminish, and after an hour, we had left the danger zone behind and were able to steer due east again. I stayed up all night, constantly alert to all the long protrusions of inlets and rocky outcrops portside. The island had no lighting at all.

We could still not use our sails with the wind blowing from the wrong direction. I oiled the propeller shaft, and on one occasion I hit the alternator in the dark engine room with the grease gun. A worrying sound rang out: an unknown object had bent the alternator cooling fan. I could straighten it out, but I had to do it in a poorly lit, hot, rolling furnace!

The continuous movement of *Message in a Bottle* meant it was a constant challenge not to bump into the ignition key or inadvertently turn on the dashboard switches. There were several incidents where the engine suddenly stalled because I fell against the key. Once in a while, the rolling and pitching sent us flying across the cabin. During one such flight, Kee landed right on the ignition key, which broke under the impact, causing the engine to fall eerily silent. I began to panic, but by great good fortune and foresight, Kee had kept a spare key. The next challenge was getting the broken piece of key out of the slot. After a lot of puzzling and fiddling, I managed; we put in the new key, and the engine started again.

We rolled on further with many bumps. The currents were strange, and we were only sailing at two and a half knots. The automatic pilot whimpered and groaned. We took turns securing ourselves on the bench to sleep. Even if we didn't manage that, simply lying with our eyes shut was refreshing. Only at night did we use the security belt tied around our waist and attached to the rings specially welded into the cabin.

We sailed in the direction of Boa Vista, another of the Cabo Verde islands. However tempting it was, we did not want to stop there but wanted to brave our way to Dakar. This was probably the most challenging part of the journey. We had to get through it as quickly as possible. It was too stressful to rely purely on the engine. The unexpectedly southern solid currents had made us drift between São Nicolau and Boa Vista, despite us having steered with all our might. We had taken a considerable detour and wasted a lot of fuel, and now we had to travel a more cumbersome route along the north coast of Boa Vista.

The island looked magnificent from a distance — large, white sandy beaches under flat rocks and some woodland here and there. In two days, we had covered 156 miles. There were still 350 miles to go before we reached Dakar. That gave us hope. We had to sail less south and more towards the east.

> *Kee: My right shoulder was in terrible pain because I had been thrown into the wall with great force. This passage was much more complicated than the one from Tenerife to Cabo Verde. High, slanted waves stormed across the portside, continually throwing us off course. Sometimes we felt like prisoners of the sea. If you have never experienced it, there is no way you can imagine it.*
>
> *Everything we had to do cost so much effort that we first needed time to muster the courage to make a start. We always felt our togetherness very intensely on the sea. We only had each other and depended on each other, although once in a while, I also called out to my dear father or mother in heaven to help us.*

That day we ate broken pieces of cracker and arrowroot biscuits, which I had collected from under the floor, stumbling and swaying. I gave them to Fons in a mug. The contents of two cans of peas and one can of meatballs became our meal, which I heated with legs spread, wiggling above the open hole above the axle. My stomach was pressed against the countertop, my bum against the wall, and the pan in my hand. We always left more than half, and that was just enough for us. In the meantime, a mass of water from breaking waves sloshed across us in the cabin, leaving seawater in our food and soaked crackers.

The clothes under the survival suits we wore at night became drenched with seawater. In the morning, we hung them onto the hooks on the back mast as soon as the temperature rose. The sun shone strongly, but the wind still made it cold. We had brought wet wipes in plastic containers, which we could use to freshen up a little. We scooped water from the sea with our small steel pan to brush our teeth, while hanging half overboard.

More and more water was appearing under the axle. How was that possible? Opening the hatch in the neck of *Message in a Bottle*, we were startled to see a lot of water sloshing about. All our materials and food were drifting around in the seawater. We pulled six large buckets full out of the neck of *Message in a Bottle*. When the neck finally dried up, I saw another trickle of water come in through a small opening where a tube for a bow thruster had once run. I found silicone glue and managed to seal the hole.

Our leakage problems meant that we had done very few miles. Currents and wind had a firm grasp on *Message in a Bottle*. Dakar was another 120 miles away. Everything was clammy, wet and filthy. We couldn't move around normally or stand anywhere. We were limp and on edge. Despite our adjustments, we had strayed too far north. We simply could not control the course because of the strange currents and winds.

Suddenly there was a clatter in the galley. The lock on the kitchen door had broken open, and the contents flew through the open floor above the propeller shaft. I stopped the engine, and Kee had to dig around under the axle for cutlery, sugar cubes, herbs and the contents from pots and plastic boxes and gather it together. It was quite a challenge to squeeze everything back into the cupboards and secure the lock before it all came crashing back out again. I made sure the cabinet could no longer be opened. We put the essentials in the container on the countertop.

When we checked our position, we were happy despite the rainstorms that now hit us. We were in the right place and heading due east at over four knots. It was not long before we saw the shimmering light from the city.

> *Kee: I saw small fishing boats around us with men throwing out or reeling in fishing nets on buoys. This meant we were close to land. Since a woman is always a woman, I made up a quick henna rinse to dye my hair to arrive new and fresh but alas pretty wrinkled in the new continent. I left the mush in my hair for half an hour before rinsing it off with buckets of seawater, hanging overboard.*
>
> *We saw low land appearing vaguely in the distance. 'Africa, here we come,' I shouted.*
>
> *Fons went to sit at the helm so he could correct our course if there were any obstacles. He looked agitated. It was tricky to work out how to sail around Île Madeleine and Île de Gorée. As if that wasn't enough, we had rough, short waves directly against us, which made the cork*

dive down deeply and repeatedly, causing us to jolt back and forth. Hours later, after the large industrial port, we spotted what we presumed to be the bay off the district of Hann on the eastern side of the peninsula. That was where we needed to be.

We saw lots of sailboat masts and were amazed they were so numerous. Attaching both anchors to ropes with great difficulty, we threw them overboard quite a distance from the other boats. They stuck. But it soon became low tide. We touched the bottom with our keel and started to lean. There were long green strands of algae drifting along everywhere, which tangled up the propeller. Fortunately, we could pull ourselves free and motor on into the port to deeper waters, where we found a safe spot.

'Africa, here we are!'

Africa Calls

Message in a Bottle

Built on a peninsula, Dakar is the capital of Senegal, which was a French colony for 300 years until 1960. Our French neighbour came by to welcome us and explain a few things. He had been staying here for years and was married to a Senegalese girl. We soon discovered that quite a few older men, primarily French, had been enjoying life on their boats for years with their young Senegalese girlfriends. The *Passeur*, a ship from the yachting club, ferried people back and forth between the boats and land. If you became a member, you could make use of a lot of facilities.

> *Kee: Our first ride through the city stunned us. Colourfully dressed women in long garments and with proud postures, carried all sorts of things on their heads, moving among the rubbish spread out everywhere and the mountains of waste. The heavy traffic moved along uneven, sandy roads into the city. We saw a mixture of fuming, blue-black, old, dented and rusty cars, often with shattered windscreens, passing each other right and left and trying to jump the queue in the endless traffic jams. Blasting mopeds zigzagged in between, honking their horns, and pedestrians had to dive aside in time to avoid getting caught under or between something.*

Senegalese people with all kinds of goods to trade, such as a metre-wide station clock, oversized underpants, fluorescent tubes and cigarettes sold individually, were walking between the queueing cars offering their goods.

There were fruit and vegetable stands everywhere and lots and lots of flies. A long plank on a frame, next to a wonky sofa or rickety chair placed under a parasol or behind a stretched curtain, made up a restaurant. These were endless. A mama dished large bowls of white or spicy rice and smaller bowls with pieces of cabbage, cassava, carrot, aubergine and fish. That was the national dish, thieboudienne.

On another market, I could get mysterious things that would somehow bring me health or happiness. I had men behind me that I could not shake off, and they used all sorts of tricks and dramas to sell me things at much too high prices. What kept surprising me was that the men just

Under engine off Dakar port

clutched or kneaded their testicles, even when I was talking
to them, and they peed anywhere they found convenient.
Dakar was indeed a feast for the eyes.

Daniel, Nina and Stijn arrived after a long and remarkable motorbike journey. They had stayed with horse breeders in Spain, and in Morocco a family had taken them in after Daniel's motorbike broke down and they had to wait for new parts. They thought Morocco was beautiful and the people amazingly hospitable. In Mauritania, they drove through the desert on a paved road to Senegal. After his motorbike broke down and he sold its parts, Stijn hitchhiked with an Australian girl whose lover was still in Australia.

They all came to live on board with us, which was a lot of fun. After being on board with us for a while, Daniel and Nina moved on to a trimaran belonging to friends we had made here. We made a habit of all getting together for breakfast at a stone table under the trees.

I was thinking about how to improve the stability of *Message in a Bottle* without too much work, and how to add bilge keels to reduce the rolling. We also had to apply anti-fouling treatment to prevent the growth and build-up of algae. Daniel offered to lend a hand with those tasks, but both meant lifting *Message in a Bottle* out of the water. As it turned out, many boats were on a waiting list to be hoisted up for refurbishment and there were only two trailers. We had no choice but to wait, which gave us the opportunity to get to know Dakar and Senegal better.

Kee: I regularly wandered through Hann, the fishing
village near where we were anchored. Every day there
was a busy fish market on the beach. There was a buzz of
activity from early morning when the trays of fish were

brought on land. Entrails and blood-covered rubbish lay piled up, and the vultures circled above. There was always a stench. The filthy open sewers released coagulated, rotting piles of filth into the sea close by, making matters worse. We would never go swimming in the bay, but many of the locals washed thoroughly in the water every morning.

In the morning, I saw people in small narrow wooden boats paddling frantically against the wind and the waves. Once in a while, they came alongside us and we'd buy a fish from them. There were people everywhere with little plastic bowls in their hands. They filled them with water to wash their hands, feet and face for their five prayer times each day. They also used them to rinse after they had relieved themselves. People sat or lay on straw mats under a tree. Men and boys washed and scrubbed their goats in the sea for sale or slaughter. Contact here was easy and informal, and we were often asked to take people back with us to Europe.

My favourite place was the passage from the market to the beach where my friend N'Dyefatou Mo sold "bin bins" (stomach chains), "pan de nuits" (transparent skirts) and "def" (aphrodisiacs). Together with scents and other items, these were the secret sex drive-enhancing substances women indulged in to keep their men for themselves, which was quite difficult around here. The men were fascinated with them. I was initiated into the rituals and demonstrated my "def" for Fons. In his case, their main effect was to make him laugh.

We had to wait for at least another month before *Message in a Bottle* could be lifted from the water for repairs and anti-fouling.

This meant our sons Robin and Brendan could come and visit us. Using public transport, we travelled with them to the green south of Senegal and Gambia. We visited villages and a bird island, and we sailed in *pirogues*, long, narrow canoes carved from a single tree trunk. The boys had the time of their lives. They visited discos where people mainly danced with themselves in front of enormous mirrors. Our boys were clothed in African shirts when they left Dakar's glow to travel back to Europe.

Since the repairs on *Message in a Bottle* were delayed, we travelled on local transport to Mali, Burkina Faso and Ghana. It was a great adventure. We did the 730 miles to Mali by bus. Every bus was dented and rusty, almost falling apart and invariably with a cracked windscreen. The door fell off one bus while it was driving; the driver just stopped, picked it up, and tied it onto the roof. We were blinded by the red dust swirling in through the open door. At one stage in the journey, the driver had to cut down a tree so that part of it could be used as a support; it was pushed under the engine so it could not fall out. Rain flowed through the leaks in the roof. The rickety, old, lopsided seats pressed their iron coils into our backs.

One night, we all slept around the bus because robbers had been sighted in the area, and we decided it was better to continue our journey in daylight. Once in a while, we had to walk next to the bus for a few kilometres until we had passed the slippery road surface full of deep holes. After four days and 1,200 kilometres of driving, we were finally in Bamako, the capital of Mali. It was a fantastic journey and we decided to continue our quest by bus.

Mali was extraordinary. In the Dogon country, we trekked on foot through tiny villages with their particular construction style along the Bandiagara Cliffs. For more than 600 years, people were isolated there, so their traditions were upheld without any change. Because of this, the Dogon culture was considered one of the most indigenous in Africa. We slept on roofs under mosquito nets. We heard the unusual greetings people exchanged at the crack of dawn. In the market in the middle of the rugged landscape, we tasted lukewarm foaming beer brewed by old women, and we took in the amazing herbs and foods and tried different things. We sweated and climbed around in the scorching heat. After one challenging climb, we descended to a waterfall, jumped into the river gorge and let the powerful current massage our bodies. We had no idea that seemingly clean water had infected us with bilharzia, a parasitic worm that damages your organs in the long run. We ended up having to go to the Institute of Tropical Medicine in Antwerp to be freed of the deadly worm just in time before it developed into a more severe disease.

We travelled to the border of Burkina Faso in a horse-drawn cart. From there, we travelled on a dilapidated bus with yet more broken windows.

Burkina Faso was much cleaner than Senegal, and despite being poor, it had well-maintained roads. There were many cafés with terraces where you could buy large bottles of beer, unlike in other Muslim countries. We travelled from Burkina Faso to Ghana by bus. Despite many warnings from Kee's sister-in-law, who lived there, we stepped into a shaky, old bus instead of waiting for the large coach. There were still hours to go to Takoradi, where Kee's brother Pedro lived. All that time, we and our fellow passengers were terrified by our driver's irresponsible driving, and we regularly saw wrecks lying by the roadside. But thankfully, we arrived in the south of Ghana in one piece and saw the Atlantic Ocean again. We saw stunningly beautiful mountains and lots of green — what a breath of fresh air after all those dry, barren countries.

*

After all the adventures back in Dakar, it was finally *Message in a Bottle*'s turn to be put onto a trailer on the beach and taken out of the water. That was done using primitive equipment like a rusty, 50-year-old winch, a leftover from the French colonists, and an equally old, beaten-up trailer. Nevertheless, it all went smoothly. The Senegalese were true experts in improvisation. Fons found suitable steel sheets and started to weld two three-metre-long bilge keels to the hull. In two weeks, the job was done.

Daniel and Nina sailed off as crew for a Swiss friend going to Brazil. They were replaced by two enthusiastic young Frenchmen, Romain and Benjamin, who had arrived hitch-hiking a couple of days earlier and asked us if we could sail together to Cabo Verde. Since we hit it off straight away, we agreed. It was hard to say goodbye to Dakar, our friends, the Senegalese and Hann. But it was good to be with Romain and Benjamin and to continue our adventure.

Our new bilge keels significantly reduced *Message in a Bottle*'s rolling motion, although I was disappointed they didn't cancel it out more. We hoisted the junk sail as soon as we were on the right course and reached Cabo Verde in five unremarkable days. In the past, we had sailed in the other direction; for us, the reversed route was better for currents and winds. We sailed into the bay and cast anchor again in Mindelo without problems. One day later, Romain and Benjamin found a catamaran with a temporarily disabled captain who needed help. They completed the crew and set off for Martinique.

We moored at the not-so-safe quay wall to make some changes on board as the long journey across the ocean was about to begin. We could sail in front of the wind for the most part, so we turned a strong but heavy second-hand mainsail into a square sail, and we bought a six-metre iron tube that would serve as a yard. On the quay, we attached the sail and the braces to the yard. We filled up with diesel and water. It was time for us to leave – it was mid-January and the turbulent winter season had started.

Barbados Bound

Message in a Bottle

During the 2,000-mile-long ocean crossing to Barbados, I intended to use the engine as little as possible. In the trade wind belt, it should be possible to sail the *Bottle* to the other side. That *Message in a Bottle* was not a smooth sailing vessel at sea was nothing new.

Keeping the vessel on course was extremely tiring if the massive waves came rolling in diagonally over starboard, and that would be the case during the voyage to the Caribbean. Fortunately, our automatic pilot was still in good shape, despite being overextended on the route to Dakar. The problem was that it used a lot of power to turn the rudder. Until now, that had been provided by the main engine, but if we did not use that power source, the batteries would not be charged. I hoped the two solar panels secured on the deck would provide sufficient power.

From experience, we knew that during the winter, we could be plagued by numerous stormy winds that produced squalls. They did not last long and were preceded mainly by a lonely dark cloud so that, during daytime at least, we could take precautions. We could, of course, be surprised by a storm at night, making it all-hands-on-deck. It would be essential to have the engine ready to keep *Message in a Bottle* on course in such a case.

We headed west to the Cabo Verde archipelago, stopping off briefly in Mindelo again. We set off once more, passing by the shelter of the island of Santo Antão. We had to defy the strong current and the waters that the north-east wind whipped up in the channel between São Vicente and Santo Antão. After this we could change the course to due west.

> **Kee:** *We were fine. There was hardly any wind, so we could place the aerial on the deck. Santo Antão still sheltered us, and for the first time,* Message in a Bottle *did not move much and had become a viable living space. We had got used to the rolling and swaying movements, which fortunately were significantly reduced after Fons welded on the bilge keels in Dakar.*
>
> *We were now headed westwards past the Cabo Verde islands and had 1,600 miles to go before arriving in Barbados.*
>
> *We washed in the tub with seawater and scrubbed ourselves using rough, African washing nets. We felt relaxed since the weather was calm. The sea changed by the moment, and I could stand dreaming for hours, looking out for dorados jumping out of the water and watching the clouds move across the sky. The sun was there every day, and at night the overwhelming twinkling and winking starry sky stretched from horizon to horizon, unique and touchingly magnificent.*
>
> *We often felt like we were the only people on Earth. Sometimes we lived with sea swallows; on other days dorados appeared around us. The schools of fish we used to see every day were no longer around, and apart from the occasional flying fish, we saw no signs of life. We were*

convinced that overfishing by floating fish factories was to blame. We had seen that the enormous cold storage facilities built on the Cabo Verde islands were deserted. The fish and the Japanese fishermen were gone, and the locals hardly caught anything now.

One triggerfish swam next to Message in a Bottle *– where were the hundreds of others? Suddenly two magnificent orcas rose out of the water close behind us. They are incredible, streamlined animals but are the enemies of almost all the other ocean inhabitants.*

This was the fourth dangerous adventure I had undertaken with Kee. She had passed her trial by fire several times, proving her resilience in the worst conditions imaginable. She had been particularly tested during our intense voyage aboard *Floating Truck* from New York to Lisbon. When everything was thrown at us with technical, meteorological and physical setbacks, Kee refused to give up even though she was frequently scared. I knew I was largely to blame for that because of my many narrow escapes on board such as when I hung under the truck above the open sea in heavy weather to check the drive shaft. What we both feared most was one of us disappearing into the waves. A chilling thought, but it could quickly happen, especially on our raft that had no railing. The sea does not give; it takes.

*

30 January. We took turns keeping watch. We felt drained, but now that we were in the middle of the ocean, we had simplified things considerably. Every half hour, we took turns to inspect if everything was in order. With a northeasterly force 3 to 4 blowing diagonally behind us, we could square the sail so that it steered *Message in a Bottle* on the automatic pilot course. That meant it did not have to work so hard and used less power.

We were 1,000 miles from Barbados. Sharks were something else we no longer saw, as we had in the past. They too were victims of overfishing, their large livers used for cosmetic purposes, and in some parts of Asia, their fins used for shark fin soup. In the past, we had encountered dead flying fish on our deck nearly every morning, but now we never did. In calm weather, we often stood looking out for friends in the water or the air. Sometimes deep underneath us, a group swam behind *Message in a Bottle*. Then, one evening, we heard drumming inside the boat. It stopped. We looked but saw nothing. Then, the drumming began again, and it turned out to be a flying fish that had flown into our galley and was squirming desperately in the container on our countertop. I seized it quickly and threw it back into the sea.

> *Kee: We admired the sea. Sometimes it was grey on the port side and deep blue on the starboard, depending on the clouds above it. In the morning, before the sun came up, the water was pink, pinkish-grey or black. The clouds were our landscapes or fantasies: long, smooth snow surfaces, icebergs on the horizon, a monster's face with an open mouth and so on. The rising sun was different each day and the most beautiful part of the day. That morning it was as though it was clinging onto the horizon with its glowing claws to pull itself up and over it. Jagged clouds were tinted deep red and then bright orange before changing into singing gold that jubilantly broke open the gates of heaven when the sun came up.*
>
> *We talked about Greek and Germanic gods, about nations of people, about insects that are tougher than people and able to survive just about anything and about how we would continue with* Message in a Bottle, *but our plans varied a lot. Sometimes we did not feel well, as old and*

restless feelings passed through us. We realised we were in a hostile environment and had to remain alert. We did not need to steer, so we didn't always keep watch. At night we sometimes slept for a whole hour before one of us had to look out to see if there was a ship around. Since we never saw any ships, we became complacent, which was dangerous.

The journey we were on was a purification of body and soul. I thought about all kinds of things I never had time to consider in ordinary life, like what happiness, love, acting, and writing meant to me. I had a lot of thoughts but found it difficult to express them in words. These were the things I wrote about in my diary.

For the first time on all our journeys, Fons faithfully wrote in his logbook every day – about our position, the wind, the ship's behaviour and the time I broke down in shrieking sobs after I had to pick up a large container full of lentils that had fallen out of the cupboard.

We were happy we had each other.

Our longitude was 51° 45' W. We were approaching Barbados much faster than we had imagined. Just before we reached the 40th latitude, the weather changed from a sluggish trade wind into an unpredictable turbulent weather pattern with threatening masses of clouds. There were stressful moments when we lowered the sail to prevent it from tearing, loosening the halyard from the wheelhouse. Then we had to square and slack the sail to let it down and pull in the flapping, banging canvas that often trailed into the sea and tie it around the yard. We quickly returned to the wheelhouse. We needed to start the engine to stay on course and avoid getting into a transverse position.

Due to the continued stormy weather, we failed to hoist the mainsail and decided to use the small junk sail in the front as a storm sail. We first had to get down the foresail on the heaving deck, rig the junk sail, tie it to the front mast, and hoist it. That worked perfectly too. Would we get any calm wind? How long would all this last? All sorts of things could still happen.

Clouds came along that we thought we could trust but suddenly caused an enormous amount of turbulence above us. Masses of water broke against *Message in a Bottle*'s side, washing across us and flowing in through a crack in the hatch, soaking my bunk on no less than three occasions.

The constant insecurity that anything could happen was eating away at us. The weather changed from bright and clear to threatening grey and then to heavy, black skies in half an hour. We could do nothing but live in the moment. We always had to be alert, and we were confronted with reality over and over again. Adding to the struggle, the automatic pilot started to malfunction unpredictably, and it was impossible to keep *Message in a Bottle* on course.

Every few minutes, the off-course signal beeped. If that failed, we would hardly be able to continue. Manual steering was impractical and could not be endured for longer than an hour. I had to steer manually following the stars, but because I was thrown off course, I lost sight of the right star, and the sail slatted because we were on the wrong course. That could only be solved by turning on the engine. Eventually, we realised the side sail, which was stretched out in the wheelhouse to prevent breaking waves washing across us, might be influencing the mainsail. We rolled it up. And yes, that was it. After that, everything went smoothly.

The trade wind was different from what we had experienced when we'd crossed this ocean before. I was doing this route for the sixth time, and it was Kee's fourth time. In the past, in the same season and on this stretch the trade wind was stable. Now even that wasn't clear. There were so many malfunctions. We could no longer rely on anything. According to the maps, it was supposed to get better when we passed the 54th longitude.

*

Day 32. We had been fidgety and impatient for a few days and longed to arrive. We wanted firm ground under our feet again. The wind had been blowing strongly for days, and we went through the water like a rocket at nearly four knots.

We often went through hell on our ocean voyages to reach our goal. That was also the case on this journey, especially on the stretch from Cabo Verde to Dakar. We had lived through the natural cycle of the ocean, the air, the weather, the sun, moon, stars and life at sea. We were very aware of our insignificance and the inexplicable mystery of life.

A group of only eight dorados kept us company — what a difference from the hundreds that accompanied us with *Seaview*. We saw a strange encounter between a group of blue and yellow-black dorados. Kee was convinced they were kissing each other. Then, suddenly they were gone. That was just as well; if they had stayed with us, they would have been caught in Barbados. Close to *Message in a Bottle*, we saw a great green dorado catch a flying fish above the water. Those flying fish were always fleeing, and birds also besieged them.

The wind was easterly and propelled us forward. The most beautiful thing we experienced this week was a complete surprise: an encounter with a ship. She suddenly lay next to us at 7am, the *UAL Europe*, a giant container ship. We had not seen her coming. I was sitting in the wheelhouse with my back towards her, and Kee was in the cabin boiling water. The ship had changed course to find out what the strange shape in the distance was. She made an enthusiastic turn close to *Message in a Bottle* with a high wave and splash from its wash. The crew on the bridge were taking photos of us. We were not the only people in the world, after all. We adjusted our course towards the east and sounded our horn. We kept watching until they disappeared behind the horizon.

In keeping with our tradition, we threw a glass bottle into the sea. This time it contained a photograph of our vessel. We hoped that someone would find it this time round. Despite throwing messages in bottles into the sea on all our previous ocean voyages, we had yet to receive a reply.

Finally, we saw a shimmering light behind the horizon. We were tired, nervous and tense when we saw the first little lights appear. We were approaching them so slowly. When the daylight broke through, we saw Barbados faintly in the distance. That meant we were very close since this was an island we always spotted late because it's low lying. We had told our friend Rusty that we would pass South Point at approximately 10am. Suddenly we heard Rusty's voice through the marine telephone. They had seen us and were racing towards us. They hurried to the Port Authority for us, where we had to complete a few formalities at the Health, Customs and Immigration Services.

Soon, *Message in a Bottle* was rocking on her anchors in the azure blue water of Carlisle Bay in Bridgetown. We were right in front of the beach and became a tourist attraction once more.

*

For months, we lived aboard our bottle in the bay of Barbados and worked on our book. Later, a cargo ship brought *Message in a Bottle* back to Europe. We flew back and waited to welcome her back to Rotterdam harbour. We had completed our journey!

Living in a Bottle

The return of *Message in a Bottle* to Rotterdam was a time of reflection for Kee and me. We had seen and experienced so much on our adventures. Designing, constructing and then sailing our extraordinary and varied ocean vessels across the Atlantic had shaped us and brought us together in more ways than we could have imagined. Each journey would always be a part of us, a celebration of our shared spirit of exploration and adventure. But these journeys had also required immense physical endurance and we still bore the scars from our escapades.

We knew the time had come to step away from our ocean voyages, but it was much harder to walk away from our beloved *Message in a Bottle*. This particular creation had always been more than just a boat to us; she was our home and our partner, and we couldn't bear to let her go. We knew we would never again cross the Atlantic in her, but we were keen to continue our life voyage together on shore.

From the moment we returned to Antwerp, Kee wanted to live onboard. She couldn't face leaving somewhere that had meant so much to us. Initially, I wasn't keen on the idea, but I soon came to understand that living on *Message in a Bottle*, while moored in Antwerp Yacht Club marina, would offer us a new way of life while allowing us to stay connected with our adventurous past. The mooring was just minutes away from two iconic maritime landmarks: the famous Harbour House, with its modern overhang designed by Zaha Hadid, and the Museum aan de Stroom (the Museum on the Stream) with its wonderful exhibits related to shipping, the sea and the port city of Antwerp.

*

So, we made the decision to live on our boat. The next step was finding a home for our one-third scale prototype of the initial high-speed *Bottle* hydrofoil. This still-working model found its perfect place in the Museum aan de Stroom (MAS), with its eclectic, pioneering maritime collection. What better location?

As our years moored in the marina progressed, we began to think of the future, both for ourselves and *Message in a Bottle*. Maintaining our floating home was not getting easier and we were not getting younger. We realised that it was time to consider a return to land-based life. But what was to become of the bottle that had been our home for almost 12 years, and part of our dreams for more than 20?

The answer arrived in 2017 when Koos Hogeweg and Lot Saldien from Stormkop sought us out, intrigued by the *Flying Bottle* prototype they'd seen at the MAS Museum, and by the discovery it had been designed and tested to break the trans-Atlantic speed record. They were also fascinated by Kee's world record as the first woman to cross the Atlantic by raft. As we showed them around our bottle home, I saw the spark in their eyes, the same spark Kee and I had when we first envisioned our Atlantic expeditions on board.

Within half an hour we realised we shared common goals. I wanted to pass on *Message in a Bottle* to new and caring owners with a purpose, and they were keen to acquire her for their educational adventure centre nearby. It was the perfect match, especially when they reassured me that I could remain her captain for life.

So, in 2018, we began transferring ownership of *Message in a Bottle* to Stormkop. At the same time we moved into an apartment near the harbour, which enjoyed wonderful views over the Schelde River, from where we set sail on our last ocean voyage in *Message in a Bottle*.

Koos and Lot supported my suggestion that Stormkop should be a school of adventure: a place for kids and dreamers of all ages who are eager to learn about the world and their potential within it. They honoured me with the title 'Godfather of Adventure'. The label made me smile, but deep down I felt its truth. Stormkop's goal is to chase curiosity – Koos and Lot are fond of saying that curiosity can save the world. This is a belief Kee and I have always shared. Our innate curiosity for life and adventure was part of why Stormkop enlisted us as intergenerational ambassadors of adventure.

We tell our stories, working with young people and with those living with challenges, because that's what we do. We are adventurers. We chase storms, we chase curiosity, we live the adventure, one voyage at a time. And we found the perfect partner in Stormkop. This place, this creative hotspot in an abandoned shipyard at the Droogdokken in Antwerp, was our own storm in the head, and is where our hearts now belong. It's a free haven, a hub for the inquisitive and adventurous, and since 2018, more than 35,000 travellers have passed through each year, enjoying workshops, events and festivals.

Message in a Bottle, too, has found a home in Stormkop. Just like us, this incredible boat has so many stories to tell – tales of her previous life as a would-be Blue Riband contender, of her repurposing and subsequent voyage across the oceans, and of the happy 11 years that followed as our floating home in Antwerp. She inspires young and old with her tales of danger and discovery, of friends made and encounters shared. Artists and writers come here, live in her, create in her. She is not just a boat; she is a source of inspiration. Kee and I remain at one with her in spirit, determined to continue the adventure on land.

But a silent storm has struck us. It's one we did not see coming. Alzheimer's hit Kee and began to take her away from me, bit by bit, memory by memory.

But we are sailors; we know how to weather storms. Kee is still here, with me. She's still the adventurous spirit, still my muse, my mermaid. I'm still her captain, her partner in sickness and in health, in storm and in calm.

We are still sailing. Our voyage isn't over. It's just a different kind of journey now; not on the sea, but in our hearts, in our minds. We're growing old, but our spirits are still young. We are here, still dreaming, still exploring. Adventure is not about reaching the destination; it's about the journey. And our journey is still ongoing. Because you don't get older until you stop chasing the storm. And we are forever adventurers, with storms yet to chase.

Acknowledgements

The Last Adventurer: Message in a Bottle is based on a book authored by Kee and myself and published in Dutch. Its title, *Zes Keer is Genoeg,* translates to 'Six Times is Enough' with a sub-title of 'Over the Ocean in Weird Vessels'. I slowly translated the pages one day at a time over the course of a year.

To acknowledge all those who have helped and joined me over the years in my endeavours would require much research and testing of memory, as well as an added chapter, since so many have been involved in our lives and adventures.

In bringing this English book to publication, the following require sincere thanks and acknowledgement. Chris and Nadia Praat in Antwerp remain dear friends from the days we were neighbours in the marina of Antwerp Yacht Club. They introduced us to Medina Publishing in the maritime centre of Cowes. Chris and Nadia helped coordinate this endeavour. They have also been a driving force to have the Southampton International Boat Show 2023 welcome *Message in a Bottle* to the event as a visitor attraction.

Thanks also go to Koos Hogeweg and Lot Saldien who help lead Stormkop in Antwerp. I'd also like to express my gratitude to everyone at this wonderful educational organisation, where *Message in a Bottle* now has her home and I also lend a hand with my stories, self-taught skills and teaching activities.

I also wish to thank Daniel Delcroix, Stijn Oerlemans along with Remi Dubuy in Amsterdam for their invaluable technical support. I recognise and thank the great City of Antwerp for providing workshop space. I remember fondly and thank Bjorn

Tore Holtet from Narvik, Norway and Frank Robertson from Oslo who served as crew on *Seaview*. Others to thank include crew members Benjamin Ployart and Romain Dedormaal from Paris as well as Wim Robberechts TV in Brussels. There are so many others.

I also have to thank the team at Medina Publishing on the Isle of Wight. Peter Harrigan and Mohammed Alsheikh visited Antwerp to meet and spend time with me, Chris and Nadia, Koos and Lot of Stormkop. Their visit and enthusiasm was instrumental in making the book a reality and bringing *Message in a Bottle* to England.

Among the impressive Medina team, I thank Rachel Hamilton, who has brilliantly edited our translated words, Alexandra Lawson for layout, Sherif Dhaimish for managing production and tight deadlines, Jeff Eamon for checking the words, Rick Bull for reprographics, Kimi Holden Huang for the cover illustration and Simon Harrop for assisting with the complex logistics to getting *Message in a Bottle* to the 2023 Southampton International Boat Show along with administrative support from Emma Dacre.

Fons Oerlemans
Antwerp, August 2023

Kee Arens on Floating Truck. *The North Atlantic Ocean, 1983.*

MID-OCEAN ENCOUNTER

From Captain A. Morris comes this report of a short interlude in the otherwise routine passage of *Burmah Peridot* across the Atlantic.

On passage from Bonny, Nigeria to the U.S. Gulf, the Chief Officer heard on the VHF shortly after 0530 hours on 25th February—'Large westbound raft on your starboard side calling the large westbound tanker.

He could see nothing but as the signal was so strong he called me and also answered the the VHF call. The raft replied saying there were two persons on board and they were sailing from Las Palmas bound for Trinidad; also that their water supply had been contaminated by sea water and could we possibly help.

At 0550 hours we sighted a very small speck on the horizon to the north of us, almost abeam, and altered course towards it. The raft had no means of steering and we finally stopped alongside it at 0648 hours, making it fast alongside. We filled the water containers and handed over some fresh provisions and fruit, though there was not much space on the raft.

On board it were thirty four year old Dutch woman, Margaretha Arena/Oerlemans and forty one year old Belgian male, Fons Oerlemans. They had sailed from Las Palmas on 13th January and we were the first ship they had sighted during the 43 days they had been drifting. The position was 13.40N 38.30 W, which is approximately 1,600 miles distant from Las Palmas and 1,400 miles from Trinidad, so they still had about another 40 days of drifting ahead of them. The woman is writing a book about the trip which appears to be sponsored by some association in Holland. The raft was named FONS.

Another crisis was overcome for them was they had lost their only spoon overboard so we put that to rights also.

They cast off again at 0720 hours and in a very short time the raft was only a speck on the horizon once more. I informed Scheveningen Radio that the Dutch raft had been sighted and that both members were safe and well.

Extract of letter from Fons Oerlemans to Captain.

'On January 13th we left Las Palmas de Gra... Canaria. We did not see a ship until now. It is our intention to go to Trinidad or Barbados. The fir... we had several thunderstorms but the raft is d... We make about 50–55 miles a day.

Margaretha is going to write a book abou... voyage. If you contact us in Antwerp we'll s... copy. We wish you and your crew a good an... voyage.'

26

Woman and Man Raft Across Ocean

Bridgetown, Barbados

A former airline stewardess and her boyfriend, claiming a record for a woman, completed a 67-day crossing of the Atlantic Ocean aboard a homemade raft yesterday, defying storms and sharks.

"I thoroughly enjoyed the trip," said Margaretha Arena, 34, of Hilversum, the Netherlands. "But I don't plan to do it again."

Women have rafted across the Atlantic Ocean before as a sport, but record-keepers said this was the first known case of a single woman completing the crossing.

Arena and her Belgian boyfriend Fons Oerlemans, 41, of Antwerp, set sail aboard their 25-foot raft of wood and steel tubes from Las Palmas, Canary Islands, on January 13, aiming for Trinidad, 3400 miles away, off the northeast coast of Venezuela.

Strong winds and currents carried them to Barbados. A Caribbean tourist haven served them to northwest of Trinidad. A Barbados Coast Guard vessel towed their raft Fons to Bridgetown Wednesday, and the two decided they had gone far enough.

Arena said 10 days into the journey they ran into stormy weather and high winds, their bit choppy currents that tossed Oerlemans off the raft.

Oerlemans said Arena helped pull him back "with some effort."

Sharks are a constant worry, the couple said.

"Initially, I thought of making the journey alone," Arena said, but she decided to have Oerlemans along because he made a similar crossing five years ago, an 82-day.

Oerlemans built a raft for that trip and also built the *Fons*, named for himself, which floats on four steel tubes in which the couple stored food. It also has a sail.

"I'm proud of what I did, but I will not go on such a long voyage again," she said.

"I learned a lot about sea life, and more importantly, about myself."

United Press

San Francisco Chronicle.

Vlotte meid

Als je je «brief uit de oceaans- zang geloven die Fons Oerlemans (41) en Margaretha Arena (34), uit Hilversum in Nederland, aan de kapitein van een langsvarend schip hebben toevertrouwd, dan stelt de passagiersvaar van een nationale ontdekkingsvrijdgeur het opperbest. In hun brief, die ten Amerikaans peraagentschap bereikte, schrijven beiden: «Na en weken varen tussen haaien en in vaak stormachtig weer stellen we van dat een behandeling, samen- gesteld uit een man en een vrouw, haast ideaal is». De man- mans en Margaretha Arena ben vermoedelijk reeds de eerste vrouw die een oceaanovervecht zi- de rug en worden één van de volgende dagen op de A... Antilles verwacht. Indie... overtocht lukt wordt Marga... de eerste vrouw die op een via Atlantische Oceaan heeft ove... stoken en wordt haar pres... wellicht opgenomen in «Guinness Book of Records».

The wood and steel raft *Fons* yesterday after it arrived in Barbados. It is seen in the shallow draught of the Bridgetown Port. *Fons* and Margaretha use their raft net once more. It was this set that helped to keep them in touch wich the rest of the world during their long crossing of the Atlantic.

STATEN ISLAND ADVANCE, Thursda...

Truckboat—

(From Page 1)

sunburn, storms and sharks, the couple used an old steam boiler to create the "Sea-View," which endured a six-month journey from Belgium to Barbados.

"This time," Oerlemans said in his thick accent, "I decided we would try something difficult."

He may get his wish. This journey spans nearly 4,000 nautical miles — not your typical Sunday drive — but that fact doesn't bother the intrepid sailers.

"I expect that we will reach Lisbon, Portugal, in about two months," said Oerlemans as he patted the side of his Dodge truck. "From there, it's onward to Paris and Amsterdam before arriving in Belgium."

It took the hydraulic mechanic four months to build the wooden raft around the truck and gas storage tanks. Oerlemans said that the truck's engine will provide the makeshift craft, and the steering wheel is connected to the raft's rudder.

"This should be just like driving, only in water," he grinned.

It won't be all smooth sailing for the three-person crew. Besides the weather difficulties, the seafarers will have to lug around 1,000 gallons of diesel fuel and dine on canned food.

"I think they're crazy," said Pat D'Angelo, whose towing company in Elm Park is helping the Oerlemans, his wife, and the third crew member, Kees Kremer, do patchwork repairs on the craft while they wait for the Kill van Kull to reopen.

"There's no way you'll catch me out in the middle of the Atlantic on that thing," D'Angelo added, "but give the man credit for trying something extraordinary."

Oerlemans is embarking on the cruise for both fun and money. The explorer will film his adventure in hopes of making a documentary film or writing a book, but he says it's the thrill of the expedition that made him want to drive across the ocean.

"I enjoy the excitement of exploration and discovery," Oerlemans said, leaning against his floating truck.

"The only advice that I got was from my mother — she said it was all right to make the trip, but to be careful," the 45-year-old sailor continued. "But she worried about the past trips, too. This craft will be a true nautical challenge, and I can't wait to get started."

Since he doesn't want to sail around the Island in order to reach Brooklyn for supplies, Oerlemans will have to wait for

De «oude» Laatste Generatie wordt op 19 maart ll. in de zuidelijke haven van Barbados binnengesleept.

BURMAH 21/2

Sailor driving home across the Atlantic in his Dodge truck

By ED BARBINI

The next time someone starts boasting about their summer vacation, tell him about Fons Oerlemans.

He's driving a truck across the Atlantic Ocean.

"Anyone can sail across the ocean," Oerlemans said yesterday. "It will be an honor to be the first to drive to Europe."

VAN GEND & LOOS

finale

OERLEMANS DITMAAL IN EEN FLES DE OCEAAN OVER

"Wat je wilt, dat moet j

THE TAMPA TRIBUNE
Sunday, July 13, 1986

Bottled Belgian plans to wing a

By DOUG COSPER
United Press International

With a penchant for the odd, Oerlemans already has "sailed" the Atlantic in a Dodge truck set on pontoons.

Bottle
From Page 1AA

The Spirit of Amsterdam:
Crossing the Atlantic in a Bottle

OP VLEUGELS DE OCEAAN OVE

UNITED STATES 1952
300 METER

DIESELMOTOR 950 PK   ORANJE ZWAAILICHT

DE FLES VAN FONS
31 METER

LUCHTINLAAT

MANGAT

PLASTIC COCKPITRAMEN TEVENS TOEGANG

INSTRUMENTENBORD

ACHTERSTE BRANDSTOFTANK 4000 LITER

SCHROEF

HULPVLEUGEL

DRAAIVLEUGEL

KOPPELING

AS DOOR BUS IN BRANDSTOFTANK

KLEPPEN

VOORSTE BRANDSTOFTANK 5026 LITER

HULPVLEUGEL

ROER

KRUISSNELHEID 68 KM PER UUR

VOL VERMOGEN VOOR LIFT 80 KM PER UUR

STILLIGGEND

ILLUSTRATIE
JOHAN VAN DIJK

NORTH
ATLANTIC OCEAN
SOUTHERN PORTION